P9-BBQ-228

Christian Ethics
for Practical Living

Christian Ethics for Practical Living

HORACE E. ORR
Late Professor of Philosophy and Religion at Maryville College

THE WESTMINSTER PRESS
Philadelphia

LIBRARY OF CONGRESS CATALOG CARD NO. 61-9350

PRINTED IN THE UNITED STATES OF AMERICA

THIS BOOK IS DEDICATED to those students at Maryville College from 1931 to 1957 whose required study of ethics under the author's instruction provided the occasion for developing many of the ideas and illustrations contained in this book.

Contents

Christian Ethics for Practical Living

Preface

In the fall of 1956, it was my privilege to return to my alma mater, Maryville College, as an assistant to the author of this book, the man under whose instruction I had done my major undergraduate study in philosophy. A few months later, I learned that others of his former students were encouraging him to put into print the parts of his lectures they had most appreciated in his course in ethics. If he undertook the task, he said, I would have to be his eyes for proofreading. Little did I realize what my consent would mean.

The summer of 1957 found the author intent on studying certain existentialist philosophers and theologians, further enriching his knowledge for teaching the few courses he maintained during his partial retirement. This meant that it was the summer of 1958 before this book began to take shape. As he wrote the chapters in longhand, he sent them to his daughter, Mrs. Thomas Allen, in Louisville, Kentucky, for typing.

When college resumed in the fall, most of the typed manuscript had been corrected by the author. What seemed like a minor illness postponed further work on the manuscript while the author gave his waning strength to the teaching he so dearly loved. Within a few weeks it was evident that the illness was more serious than had been thought at first. On November 1, 1958, he concluded a thirty-eight-year teaching career at Maryville College, to continue, in the realm of spirit (as I'm sure he was convinced), some larger labors according to the interests and abilities for which this earthly life had been the beginning.

The manuscript of this book as it stood at that time was tentatively accepted by the publisher. However, the inevitable editing and revising remained to be done in order to meet the publisher's standards for a book acceptable to the reading public. At the request of Mrs. Orr and her children, I agreed to try this task which would be a more formidable one than that of simply proofreading. Having agreed in all good faith, I found fulfillment delayed for more than a year because of the family commitments and increased college duties which the author's passing brought to me. To the extent that my rewording and editing has made it possible for the publisher to make the author's thought available to the public, I am deeply humble and grateful. To whatever extent my hand has altered the author's intent or obscured the flavor of his expression, I apologize. The hundreds of Dr. Orr's former students who read this book will no doubt recognize his style. Others will at least be introduced to a small part of the wisdom and spirit of a man who was cherished by many generations of students at Maryville College.

As indicated above, this book grew out of lectures used by the author through the years as he taught ethics at Maryville College. (The course in ethics is required of all students for graduation.) As a Presbyterian church-related college, the ethics course assumed the validity of Christian ethics. As a liberal arts institution, the subject has been taught in the context of philosophy rather than theology or Biblical studies. And since Maryville is a small college interested in preparing young people for life and living, ethics has been considered not merely philosophical theory but also practical action. These three points of view, as the author taught them, are also evident in the following chapters, chapters the author often refers to as " studies."

The above facts will also help to explain a purpose of this book as contrasted with many other books on the general subject of morals and ethics. The author was certainly aware of and informed of the writings of other Christians in this field in recent years, even though he did not refer to many of them by name.

And while he did not seek to minimize the importance of the writings of others, he did not share many of their views. The first few chapters — especially the first — will indicate to the informed reader certain basic differences in the approach to the Bible and ethics from the views expounded by many prominent theologians. To persons who are acquainted with the existentialist approach in modern philosophy and theology, it will be evident that the author — in the interest of consistent reasoning — rejects as inadequate for immediate, practical living any theory in which knowledge of the good and right must be gained in ways radically different from those ways by which other kinds of knowledge are gained in everyday life.

But in spite of such philosophical and theological backgrounds, this book is intended not for the scholar in theory but for the intelligent layman in such matters. It is intended as reading material for the Christian who wants to think practically, yet soundly, concerning certain moral problems that he *must* face and *solve* in today's American society. These studies may find use as discussion topics for both young people and adults in college or church, although no questions or discussion guide are offered, since this is not a textbook.

In short, this book is intended for a wider audience in something of the same intent that the author had in his long years of teaching philosophy, religion, Bible, and Christian education to young people seeking liberating knowledge in the context of the Christian faith. The only reward that the author might desire from the reader is that which he frequently expressed during a lifetime devoted to his love of teaching: an attentive mind and a courteous "Thank you; now I see" when some new insight is gained. The closing chapter — indeed, the closing words — are indicative of the author's optimistic hope that the reader will make such a response by growing not only in moral insight but also in more Christian living.

A. Thomas Horst

Maryville, Tennessee

CHAPTER I

Religious Faith and Morals

MORAL IDEALS are ideals for conduct in the field of man's relation to man — the standard or goal by which a man seeks to guide and judge his interpersonal relations. Religion is concerned with man's relation to God. Moral ideals and religion can hardly be separated. Religion involves all of living; so also do morals. The word "moral" has at least two usages. It is used as opposed to amoral or nonmoral to indicate conduct that lies within the realm of free choice. It is used as opposed to immoral to indicate those choices of conduct which are good or right. The context indicates the meaning intended.

Since all of living involves a program of action, we observe that religion supplies motivation for *right* action. Moral action in turn quite often provides the basis on which we judge the sincerity of religious professions. If one professed religious faith and had very low moral standards, he would likely be considered a religious hypocrite by his neighbors. But at the same time, even a little reflection makes us aware that moral standards differ widely among sincerely religious people. Some Christians strongly disapprove of certain conduct which other Christians approve, or at least allow. Where such differences of moral standards occur, a layman finds difficulty in resolving them and often falls into dispute with his brethren.

In the first three chapters, we will discuss certain basic considerations that affect our thinking in such matters.

We must begin by frankly admitting that all Christians do not agree as to what is proper conduct in any given situation. It is easy enough to see — and agree — that some courses of action are practical in certain situations which are not practical in others; it is easy to grant that the social duty of a Christian ought to be judged in the light of the circumstances. The impossible is never required. The trouble in differences is deeper than that. For even if a certain general program of social conduct could be agreed upon by all as being *possible,* it would still be impossible, as things stand, to get *all* to agree that it was *necessarily required* of Christians. Thus, the irreligious may say, "Why don't you Christians get together?" And the religious person may feel strongly that they really should be expected to do so. He may feel frustrated because Christians cannot get together on such matters.

REASONS FOR DISAGREEMENT

At least two main reasons can be offered when disagreements occur among Christians over questions about what is right and wrong in the field of morals: one is social; the other arises out of the way different Christians interpret the Bible. Let us examine these briefly.

In the first place, social conditioning causes differing interpretations of moral duty. We accept as fact that the only way to serve God is by serving man. God, as God, needs no human help. He needs our help only at the point of his will for men. But when we attempt to determine moral and social requirements in the light of men's needs, we quickly recognize another fact. Men's ideas about what other men need — that is, what is really good for them — arise largely out of a process of social conditioning.

This does not mean that social conditioning is the *only* source of moral judgments. Many ethical writers rightly insist that a feeling one has within himself regarding the relation of an action toward truth — its conformity to what is real — is also present. Still, we must recognize that in a large part of the modern world social conditioning *is* regarded as the only source of moral judgments. This is true, for example, in the Communist world. Following the implications of psychological experiments of Pavlov, who was able to produce the same physical reaction through a wide variety of differing stimuli, many people logically conclude that men can be made to want, and so to do, what an absolute authority requires of them.

While we may reject the sweeping conclusion of such an example, we have to admit that social conditioning has much to do with moral judgment everywhere. In time of war, Christians of one nation might feel religiously justified — even obligated — on account of the social conditioning we call patriotism to perform acts that equally devout Christians in an opposing nation would regard with horror. Social conditioning has important bearing upon the values that people cherish and wish to see embodied in life and in their social institutions. Thus, the American people desire to see *their* form of democracy strengthened and made permanent. They are likely, too, to believe strongly in what they may call our form of the "people's capitalism." But there are other Christians with differing background and experience who desire to see some other social, economic, and political ideals made permanent.

It seems unlikely that we can expect people of completely differing social background to come to agreement regarding moral duty; so clashes do arise among Christians over the moral requirements of religious faith. Recognition of these facts will not necessarily bring Christians into closer agreement regarding moral duty but may provide a more fruitful area of discussion than if these facts were ignored. The fact remains true that we cannot separate Christian living from moral duty. And Christian living means not only the worship of God but also the serving of God through meeting the needs of fellow men according to the will of God. Mention of "the will of God" presents us with another problem.

A second cause for differing interpretations of moral duty among Christians arises out of the different ways in which they interpret the Bible. That this is a source of moral problems is well known. At least three ways of interpretation are common.

One sincere Christian thinks the moral injunctions of the Bible should be taken in the most literal sense possible — the commands are the actual word of God. Little explanation need be given to understand this view. The words are in black and white just as God gave them to men. If one can read, he can read what God demands in human conduct.

Another Christian, equally sincere, may see the situation otherwise. He believes God will make moral duty clear if the Christian reads his Bible devoutly and if he humbly seeks to know what his moral duty is. Present-day moral duty may be something different from what is actually written in the Bible. It may be different, also, from what one's own unaided reason would suggest in the circumstances. Moral duty may not be the written word of the Bible as such, neither necessarily the meaning intended by the inspired writer as he wrote for the situation in his own day. Rather, moral duty is the meaning of the Bible which God reveals *now* through the Holy Spirit to a man in a *present* need of moral guidance.

Obviously, these are two different ways of looking at this matter, and quite different results may follow in human conduct. But there is still a third way of looking at the insights for moral guidance which are found in the Bible.

This way understands that the moral insights found at different times and in differing circumstances must be interpreted in the light of those times and circumstances. It holds that the work of the Holy Spirit is not to supplant but to guide one's intelligence toward a better understanding of moral duty. The guidance is, in one respect, like that which a traveler experiences. A numbered, well-marked highway is guidance toward one's destination — not a description of the destination. When one enters upon the highway, the city to which he is going may be a long distance away, but if followed faithfully, the highway will lead him to the city he seeks.

This third view is adopted in these studies. This view seems consistent with the idea that moral insight grows as understanding increases and that moral duty changes with the growth of understanding. It is consistent also with the view that *total* living is morally significant — all of life's relationships, including the physical, social, economic, intellectual, and political, as well as the religious.

Since our conclusion is not the one followed by many current writers in the field of Christian ethics, this conclusion needs a further brief justification in order to have agreement with the reader as we go forward in these studies.

THE BIBLE AS AUTHORITY IN MORALS

When we come to consider the authority of the moral injunctions found in the Bible, two principles must be kept clearly in mind: the Christian cannot be indifferent to moral requirements and still regard himself a Christian; and the Christian professes to accept the Bible — in some sense — as the word of God.

In considering the first of these principles, we mean to say that there is such a thing as Christian conduct. For the Christian, this is what is meant by "good," as God requires good. The real question then is this: Is this good conduct binding on the Christian because it is required in the Bible? Or does the Christian expect to find moral guidance in the Bible because the Bible contains directive principles which, properly applied, are good and right in the very nature of things? If one affirms the first alternative, he is saying that moral precepts are binding because they are required in the Bible. If the second is affirmed, he is saying that the Bible is regarded as containing the directive principles which it does primarily because such principles are true and accurate guides to the good life.

The important thing to notice is that in either case this is true: there *are* Christian ways of moral action and the Christian will seek to be guided by them. But more than that, the Christian will consider himself under God's judgment with respect to such moral standards.

This is one thing that must be kept in mind throughout any discussion of the relation of the Bible to moral conduct. The other, as stated above, is the fact that a Christian, by his being a Christian, professes to accept the Bible as the word of God. Some of the various ways in which this profession is understood will be noted now. Really, in one's thinking, this principle must come before the one discussed in the paragraph above. Obviously, how one considers the Bible to be the word of God will condition his understanding of the way in which the Bible's moral injunctions are binding upon him. So the ideas now to be discussed are of prior importance. They are placed second in our discussion because they require a somewhat longer statement.

At the start of this discussion, it would be well to remind ourselves that the distinguishing mark of religion in anyone's life is his religious way of living. The distinguishing mark of religion is not mere belief in God's existence but rather a living embodiment of the difference God makes for the lives of those who believe. That this is so for the Christian might be indicated in the statement, " For as the body apart from the spirit is dead, so faith apart from works is dead " (James 2:26).

But a religious way of living requires a source from which one may discover what is expected in this way of living. That source is, for the religious person, his revelation. His revelation is his guide toward the good — the good which his religion can bring him. Every person then, in being religious, is committed to a religious regard for some kind of revelation of the good — committed to something that somehow represents the voice of God; committed to the guide that leads a man toward those benefits he may gain by living in accordance with God's will. For the Christian, this something — this guide, this revelation — is the Bible.

It follows that anyone who professes to believe in a Christian civilization professes at the same time to believe the Bible to be, in some sense, the inspired word of God. This much is required by the definition of religion. Hence, when professing Christians are not agreed (as often happens) on the manner in which moral guidance is obtained from the Bible, there is no need to argue (as also often happens) whether or not one or the other rejects the Bible as God's word. Neither can do that. By professing to be Christian, one professes he accepts the Bible. And it is quite futile to argue that one does *not* believe what he declares he *does* believe.

The question is — and it remains as we stated above — In what sense and to what extent does the Bible, as it stands, describe the way God has acted in history? This is important because in this sense and to this extent the Christian is provided insight for guidance in the field of morals.

In answering this question, Christians tend in general to fall into three groups, as we have said. The view of each group needs to be stated briefly in order to make clear the relation of the Christian religion to the concept of moral judgments that is being advanced in these chapters.

The Bible as Literal History

One group of Christians takes the Bible more or less literally. Persons in this group believe that the Bible is a record of events in history. The acts described therein as acts of God are understood as *real* acts of God. They represent his sovereign will and wisdom at the time they came to pass. Any moral insights or judgments found in these acts must therefore be interpreted in this light.

Without attempting to argue fully this point of view, it must be pointed out that grave difficulties are encountered from the standpoint of moral guidance. One such difficulty appears when, in two different places in the Bible, God appears to give contradictory moral judgment concerning the same action. For example, in II Kings 10:30 we read this: "And the Lord said to Jehu, 'Because you have done well in carrying out what is right in my eyes, and have done to the house of Ahab according to all that was in my heart, your sons of the fourth generation shall sit on the throne of Israel.'" But a later writer, Hosea, referring to the same historical event, said: "And the Lord said to him, 'Call his name Jezreel; for yet a little while, and I will punish the house of Jehu for the blood of Jezreel, and I will put an end to the kingdom of the house of Israel. And on that day, I will break the bow of Israel in the valley of Jezreel'" (Hos. 1:4–5).

If these two Bible writers are understood literally, it would appear that God changed his moral judgment. What is written by Hosea seems to pronounce Jehu's actions wrong in the light of later historical events known to him. Not only do these passages contradict each other, but to resolve the conflict would seem to require contradicting another Biblical teaching about God's character: that God is unchangeable.

Instances are numerous where this difficulty appears with respect to moral judgment upon such practices as slavery, polygamy, temperance, war, and the like. Of course, it can be argued that some of these difficulties can be explained in the light of the infinite and timeless characteristics we attribute to God. But while this is possible, one who so argues would have to take refuge in the idea that the divine will and wisdom is not only sovereign but also may be inscrutable.

Other difficulties also appear. Such a literal understanding of the Bible makes arbitrary commands the basis of its authority to us in judging morals. And beyond this, one must be willing to accept such authority without question when it appears to guide in a direction contrary to the way things are in the universe. One is also faced with the problem of establishing the claims of one professed revelation as more valid than other professed revelations — if moral guidance is to be more than mere personal preference and if one would claim universality for the moral guidance of the Bible. Finally, it would seem that universal conformance to moral law would be dependent upon universal religious uniformity. And while such religious uniformity may be possible, the need for universal moral principles is too great and too urgent to wait upon the realization of such a possibility.

For these reasons, at least, we reject this view of the Bible. It does not seem adequate as the basis for our understanding the relation of Christian faith to moral obligation. Let us, then, turn to another way of looking at the Bible.

The Theology of the Word

One important group of modern thinkers reject the view stated above. They do so for the reasons given and for many others. Their reasons all grow out of a very careful study of the Bible and what it seems to testify concerning itself. These Christians start with the fact that the Bible claims to be the word of God. In the light of this claim, they say the Bible as a whole ought to be allowed to testify concerning itself. This point of view has often been associated with the term "theology of the word."

Obviously, the comprehensive knowledge of the Bible that is here required demands considerable study. Hence, this method of approach has done much to restore interest in the Bible as such. Thus it has provided extremely important insights. Especially has this view done much to promote a revived interest in religion among intellectuals who would find objectionable on intellectual grounds the first method discussed above. The method now under discussion *does* make the study of the Bible appear more intellectually respectable. We are interested, therefore, in this important point of view as it has been brought to bear on the subject of our concern in morals.

Beginning with the fact that the Bible claims to be the word of God, thinkers with this view believe that what is found in the Bible may *become* the word of God by the power of the Holy Spirit; the Bible writings themselves are not the divine word. Obviously, the "word of God," as the expression is used in this connection, does not refer to what is found written in the Bible — not as the words are written there. How the words of the Bible are to be understood is discussed in the next paragraph. What is meant by the "word of God" is the revealed meaning *today* for the guidance of the sincere seeker as he seeks guidance in the particular situation in which he finds himself. Thus, the sovereign God — through the Holy Spirit — intervenes in the seeker's search, transcends the seeker's natural ways of knowing, and makes clear to him what his duty is. The "word of God," then, is the meaning God is able to convey to the seeker by intuition. The meaning is the eternal truth of God seen in its application to the present situation.

Some would speak of this intuition of truth as Plato wrote of reminiscing ultimate truth. Plato (427?–347 B.C.) contended that one's knowing the real *form* of truth was possible because of one's experience with truth in a previous existence. In one's search for truth in this present existence it was possible to receive a direct insight of the truth. The present search was the occasion for, not the cause of, the intuition. The cause of the truth lay in the fact that man's mind comes equipped with a form, or pattern, by which to judge the truth which came to the mind from a previous state of existence.

In some similar way, some thinkers today would say that man's spirit can be thought capable of a sort of recollection of spiritual truth brought with him from a precreation perfect state with God. The search of the Bible is the occasion for the Holy Spirit's making possible the insight.

The words contained in the Bible must, in this case, be understood in some other way than as the direct cause of, or direct conveyor for, truth. We have to regard words as symbols whose meanings are always conditioned by our past experiences. Therefore, no words can express all God means to convey through revelation. So we have, first, the revelation of God's truth in the words of the Old Testament. Then God's meaning is embodied in the life, death, and resurrection of Christ. The words of the New Testament were then written to make clear the meaning of that embodiment. Finally, the work of the Holy Spirit today makes clear what God's word is for life and salvation. This activity of the Holy Spirit imparts this clear understanding in some way (as suggested above, or in some other way) beyond the usual limits of human meanings for words.

While not agreeing completely with this point of view of the Bible as the word of God, I can see some value in it. It has been important and helpful for a better understanding of the Bible as a *progressive* revelation. I agree that the Bible is best understood as God's revelation which shows progression as the minds of men were able progressively to understand the mind of God. But in spite of such value, this point of view is not consistent thinking. It is not consistent to reject a literal approach to the record of events recorded in the Bible and at the same time accept the idea of unconditioned intuition as the way by which truth is known (or in the field of morals, as the way by which the right is known). As indicated above, the approach to the Bible as literal history leads one to conclude that God's will is not only sovereign but also inscrutable in regard to our understanding of physical laws and moral precepts. The "theology of the word" leads one to conclude that God's will is sovereign and inscrutable in regard to our understanding of the laws governing mind and truth. The rejection of the former and acceptance of the latter is not consistent thinking. Moreover, it does not greatly help to defend the latter view (as some of its defendants do) by claiming that objection to the literalist approach is not the miracles attributed to God in the Bible, nor the acts of questionable morals such as already referred to, but the objection that God never really intended "word of God" to be understood literally as a great many orthodox Protestants have understood it. Such objection simply asserts that the *new* understanding has been received in some way beyond the *usual* limits of human meaning for words as the Holy Spirit imparts and denies that the older understanding of orthodox Protestants has had the Holy Spirit's direction. Assertions and denials such as these are difficult to argue, as is the validity of most knowledge arrived at by some form of intuition.

In any event, the field of moral requirements is one of such immediate and practical consequence that it seems impossible to wait for final decisions regarding such matters as this. Furthermore, a system of morals is needed that is universally binding, regardless of theological agreement or disagreement—even if *no* theological agreement is reached. This is not, however, to suggest that a valid moral system be divorced from religion. Morals need the grip that is provided by religious sanction. The average man needs to feel that a moral precept is not only humanly wise, but also that it is right according as he expects to be judged before God. Especially is this needed when a moral precept cuts sharply across what a man is *disposed* to do.

The Word of God Is Love

We come now to consider a third way in which the Bible is understood to be God's word and a way in which religion is related to morals. This is the approach of the chapters that follow. The Bible is the "word of God" in the sense that the essential truth found therein is this: goodness and love are at the heart of the universe. Moral laws, therefore, are binding because they are in harmony with the universe. These statements are purposely oversimplified. Their meaning will become clearer as we proceed.

Our human understanding of God's will—God's ways of acting in the universe—we express in terms of laws as we come to experience the universe as law-abiding. The ways of God with regard to human relations and of God's judging human activities are what we mean by moral laws. Moral laws, therefore, are binding because they are in harmony with the laws of the universe. They are no less real than physical laws, such as the force of gravity. True, moral and spiritual consequences do not register with the same immediate impact as the physical laws. Men may disregard moral laws for longer periods of time without conscious awareness of the tragic consequences of doing so. But the laws and consequences are nonetheless real.

Moral truths are insights that arise out of social relations where a basic faith exists that the universe is friendly to goodness and love. That the universe is friendly to goodness and love is a faith, not a scientifically provable fact. It is not possible to fit all the data at hand into this conclusion. This fact is, however, the credible faith that God made clear to writers of the Bible who contemplated the meaning of events in their time. They stated these meanings in terms of the best understanding they had of the way ultimate goodness and love operate in such life situations as they had recorded.

The increasing understanding of this principle of goodness and love at the heart of things, together with the deepening insights into what this means for men and nations, is the truth — the "word of God" — as the Bible contains it. As we today try to understand the "word of God" expressed in the Bible, difficulty is sometimes experienced, especially in the Old Testament. The most troublesome parts are not those which record God's direct interference with what we call natural laws, but those which record acts of God which are offensive to present-day moral sensibilities. These acts cease to be troublesome when we take them as good (or right) as men *at that time* were able to understand the good. For example, in the Genesis story of Abraham's intended sacrifice of his son in order to prove obedient devotion to God, one can imagine that young Isaac would have tried to escape had he known what was intended. And who could blame him? But this narrative marks a tremendous progress in the practical application of religion *as Abraham understood it*. The story recounts the necessity of loyalty to God *as one sees it*. But the progress is seen as the story shows Abraham's first clear awareness that God's nature does not demand such bloody evidence of religious devotion as Abraham had intended for his son.

The Bible thus understood means then that the morally right consists in doing the best that is possible in the circumstances according as one's knowledge and understanding have enabled him to know the good. What Abraham proposed in the sacrifice of his only son was right so far as his background, experience, and understanding made it possible for God to reveal the right to him at that time. The same was true of his owning slaves or having more wives than one. By the same token, we would say that such acts would be right for other men in exactly the same circumstances and with the same capabilities — if such a situation can be imagined.

This way of understanding the morals of the Biblical persons as sanctioned by God is harmonious with what we know of the laws governing the relations between persons. The relations of persons are based on, and limited by, what they have in *common* — language, culture, experience, and the like. Persons come to have common ideas, ideals, and hopes as a result. Fellowship, communion, and harmony are all based on what is held in common. Beyond what is held in common there is no community between persons. And since the Bible refers to God as a person, it follows that men must be in some degree like-minded with God in order to know him and be in harmony with him. Here, in passing, is a cue for understanding why a forgiving spirit is necessary in order for a man to be forgiven by God. (See Matt. 18:23-35.) It also gives significance to the passage that enjoins men to be perfect as God is perfect. (See Matt. 5:48.)

It follows that if the inspired writers were in harmony with God when they wrote (as we believe they were), then what they wrote was pleasing to God as he looked upon men in the circumstances surrounding them. What was written about God (and the ways of God) was pleasing to God. The fact that the writers were in rapport with God establishes it. And we can no more deny the writers' claims to being in harmony with God than we can deny all such claims in history — including our own.

MEANINGS AND SYMBOLS OF MEANINGS

A brief discussion of words and their meanings will serve now to explain further the point of view presented above and to conclude the purpose of this chapter. The way that is presented for looking to the Biblical narratives for guidance in morals coincides with the way in which we acquire knowledge about other things. The contrast to the intuitive method should be obvious. We learn by experience what we regard as the truth in such areas as science, history, politics, and practical affairs. In the same way we learn the meanings for which words provide the symbols. The "theology of the word" correctly insists that words are symbols and that words cannot convey meaning beyond that which is provided by the experiences of one who hears the words. In explaining the meaning of a new word — or truth — we must do so by something already having meaning to us. One may explain a fragrance by saying that it smells like a rose. Some understanding is thus conveyed by using the word symbolizing a rose. But if the fragrance is not *in fact* the fragrance of a rose, the meaning is not completely identical. An area of meaning will remain which the expression " like a rose " will not convey. Thus, I have often said to students: " I cannot tell you what I mean. I can only tell you what *you* mean by the words I use." Words as symbols of meaning fall short of their full intent in the mind of a speaker or writer. The meaning arising out of the hearer's or reader's experience with the words — this is all the meaning that can be conveyed.

Immanuel Kant spoke a truth when he said that the senses cannot *" think "* anything. Equally true is it that the mind cannot *" intuit "* anything. For this reason we have agreed that moral insights in Biblical times have progressed. They grew toward complete embodiment in Christ as men's experience with moral truth increased. Likewise, since their embodiment in Christ, moral insights have grown in the minds of sincere seekers after the full meaning of that embodiment. Insights have grown as men have found them in the midst of the growing, changing, complex meanings that arise out of living in our present-day world.

We reiterate that all this does not mean that morals can, so to speak, secede from religion. Morals cannot. On the contrary, in addition to providing the individual with a strong and necessary motivation for moral living, religion also gives a new dimension to morals. We may call the dimension " depth." By this I refer to the fact that the religious man fulfills his moral obligations under the guidance of a profound conviction that eternal consequences are involved, not simply present temporal effects. The Christian man lives in the light of an eternal destiny, which includes not only himself but also all mankind. He lives, in short, under the judgment of God upon himself and upon history.

But this does not constitute the only connection between morals and religion for the Christian. The Christian man also cherishes virtues whose validity is not necessarily borne out in individual cases of social experience in terms of rewards. He believes, for example, in kindness, self-sacrifice, patience, and the like. Often the only apparent reward for practicing such virtues is an inner conviction that the Christian ought to act in such ways. They are virtues taught by the Bible and embodied in the example of Christ. The rewards for such actions may not be a long and prosperous life — certainly these virtues did not work for Christ in such a way. But there *are* areas of living in which these virtues do work. These virtues represent applications of the great principle of love — and love does work. Love as a guiding principle works in the home. It works between man and man, among small groups of men. Thus some areas of experience — although not all individual cases — provide the basis for a divine insight that love is a cohesive principle; that love can, and ultimately must, bind all men together. Love as a cohesive principle is no less real as a fact of human social relations than a physical principle of cohesion is a fact of the world of nature. To these facts we shall return in succeeding chapters. This principle of love in social relations is recognized as a fact when Christians refer to the "Fatherhood of God and the brotherhood of man." The Christian further accepts the supremacy of the principle of love when he acknowledges that God is love and quotes the insight of the New Testament writer: "For love is of God, and he who loves is born of God and knows God" (I John 4:7).

In sum then, morals cannot do without religion. At the same time, religious insights into what is moral cannot be divorced completely from experience. Truth in this field of morals is arrived at through experiences in human relations. But insights in morals grow as one views his human relations in the light of a basic act of faith (which in a practical sense is religion). This act of faith is an assurance that the universe is so constituted that friendliness to good can be relied upon as true in the nature of things. Christian moral living can be described as the orientation of all of life in the light of this principle.

CHAPTER

II

Moral Growth

Two things are apparent from what has so far been said. One is that an element of faith lies back of our reasoning in morals. The other is that we should expect moral growth in both persons and society. The previous chapter briefly stated our point of view with regard to religious faith and the Bible as they relate to morals. The present chapter will examine our point of view regarding moral growth. In this chapter (as in the next) we shall be concerned with certain facts and ideas derived from the philosophical study of ethics while seeking to relate these to a Christian religious view.

SOME BASIC ASSUMPTIONS OF MORAL INQUIRY

The idea of growth in morals is but one of several basic assumptions in the philosophical inquiry of ethics. Furthermore, the manner in which moral growth takes place is variously conceived. Consideration of some of these assumptions and the particular ethical theory that we espouse is therefore the outline of the first part of this chapter.

Ethical Postulates or Assumptions

Even apart from any religious study of morals, there is a necessary element of faith involved wherever a standard is sought for moral conduct. We simply assume that certain principles — sometimes called "ethical postulates" — are true. While it would be beyond the scope of our intent to discuss and justify the various postulates usually proposed by writers on ethics, some brief statements will give perspective to our consideration of moral growth.

One common postulate is that change for the better is possible in human conduct. If this fact were not so, there could be no reason (except a historical one) for giving time to a study of morals. This principle also implies what is sometimes considered another postulate: that people — moral agents — can either perform or leave unperformed acts leading toward improvement. Again it can be argued that unless something of this ability of choice of action is present, it is useless to give attention to a study of morals.

In a similar way we must assume further that it is possible to pass a permanent moral judgment on a given act so long as the circumstances involved in the act remain substantially unchanged. Unless this is so, nobody has a right to pass a moral judgment on the acts of another person. And unless this quality of permanency is valid, it would be senseless to think of an act, as such, as being morally good or bad; it might change from one moment of time to the next. A fourth postulate assumes a kind of permanency in the moral quality of acts, but it is persons, not time, which are of the essence. We must assume that persons — as persons and without qualifying adjectives regarding circumstances — are equal. It can be argued here that if this were not so, it would be impossible to pass an objective moral judgment and say that persons — regardless of race, social status, etc. — ought to act according to it.

That assumptions such as these are a starting place should not be surprising. These postulates underlying the study of morals are, in some respects, not unlike the assumptions with which one must begin a study of a physical science. A difference, of course, exists in that a physical science is a descriptive science, while a scientific study of morals is for normative purposes. But in the descriptive sciences, just as indicated in morals, thinking has to start with certain things taken for granted. In any science it must be taken for granted that the mind is capable of arriving at truth, that is, that certain things which seem to be correct are in fact correct. If we experiment in a physical science, as in chemistry for example, hoping to arrive at general conclusions, we must assume also that the parts of a whole used for experimentation may be taken to represent the whole correctly. No progress at all would be possible in the physical sciences without such assumptions as these. And these are assumptions! — assumptions which in our scientific age we have come to take so much for granted that we scarcely think of them as such.

The point we are making and its relation to our study is this: if we reason at all, we cannot escape assumptions. And nobody has a right to dismiss morals as purely subjective (or else as purely authoritarian) on the ground that such a study must begin with postulates. For the same reason one would have a right to dismiss conclusions in the physical sciences as being unwarranted, but seldom does one do so if he is concerned for practical living!

Moral Progress or Growth

The matter of moral growth is suggested and included under the first postulate stated above — the possibility for improvement in morals. Some further discussion is necessary as to the reality of moral growth and the manner in which it takes place. Is there really evidence in the past upon which to base this assertion that moral improvement is possible? The question is often put this way: "Has there been moral progress in the past? Are our times better than the old times?" Does the answer "yes" to such questions mean that we are, on the whole, better men than our grandfathers and great-grandfathers were?

This sort of questioning gives us pause for several reasons. We often talk about "the good old times." And when we do, older people are the ones most likely to feel that the old times were better. Their years of experience would seem to provide them with a basis for this kind of comparative judgment. But not infrequently younger persons challenge the validity of this kind of conclusion. They suggest that what we are accustomed to has a bearing on what we like and approve. So in regard to moral progress — or lack of it as seen by an older person — it might well be because our times and our ways are *our* times and *our* ways. Proof is abundant that it is the nature of people to adjust themselves to what they have. We like our own homes, our own food, our own friends. Woe betide the " meddling do-gooder from the outside " who seeks to improve us! It could be, then, that so-called progress in morals is mere change which we like because we are a part of the change. Certainly it is possible to argue this point.

Or one might question in another way. Doesn't the situation in our world prove that the world becomes progressively *worse* morally? Never before has there been so much war and threat of war. Never before have the horrors of war been so great and all-inclusive in prospect as now. And what about crime and delinquency and the divorce rate? What about the prospective spread of an atheistic, revolutionary economic and political system that threatens to engulf the whole earth? — unless, of course, we are able to halt its spread by unleashing atomic power, which in turn would probably result in the destruction of the race itself. When such facts are faced and the question asked, " Is mankind making moral progress? " isn't the answer an emphatic " No! " or at the very least a grave " I doubt it "?

Such discussion is not intended to deny the postulate of the possibility of moral growth. Rather, in the light of such considerations as these, we would infer that moral progress is not automatic. We are not on an escalator of progress in this field. If progress has been made — and it has — it has not been without human effort. If progress can yet be made, it is possible that it should not be automatic. Rather, we — persons, moral agents — must bring it about. It is my conviction that we can do just that.

Furthermore, I believe that we are likely to judge the general question about moral progress too narrowly. Before negative answers are given to the questions as suggested in the paragraphs above, we should include in our judgment an answer to such other questions as these: Has there been an increase of knowledge about the world and the laws governing it? Has it become possible to have a fuller realization of the intellectual, social, and spiritual capacities of mankind? Has the ability become greater to master destructive and evil forces in nature and life? The answer to these questions must be considered. To whatever extent an affirmative answer can be given — and an affirmative answer can be given — progress must be held to have been real in the past.

Moreover, regardless of the judgment one may pass on the present social order — as a social order — it remains possible for the individual — as a person — to make progress. This is so because of the vastly increased potentialities for good (as well as for evil) of persons as persons. That such an increase for good is possible is proved through recent years by the control which persons have brought about over natural forces and such powers as world-wide communication.

Such conclusions — that moral growth is possible in individuals as persons — bring us to a statement of the ideal toward which progress should be made.

Perfectionism as Basic Moral Theory

At this point we enter the field of ethical theory back of such ethical postulates as we have stated above. There are a number of such theories: formalism, utilitarianism, naturalism, and the like. Each theory attempts to establish its ideal by which moral progress is judged. It would be of value to examine these and other theories — their history and the reasons advanced for and against them. This is done at considerable length in college classes in ethics, and the interested reader can consult any of several textbooks designed for this purpose. (See, for example, Thomas E. Hill, *Ethics in Theory and Practice;* The Thomas Y. Crowell Co., 1956. Charles H. Patterson, *Moral Standards,* second edition; The Ronald Press Company, 1957.) However, for our present purposes we must confine ourselves to some statements about the perfectionist theory that we are adopting in these studies as setting forth the best goal toward which a system of morals can move. I am convinced that perfectionism can include the best of what is to be found in the other theories.

Perfectionism had historical predecessors long before the beginning of the Christian era in Greece. The idea was stated in terms of self-realization. The goal of moral conduct was thought to be that which most completely satisfies the demands of human nature, i.e., a realization of the self. We note significantly that Greek thinking always limited itself to the present life; the good had to find justification in the here and now.

The formulation of this idea of self-realization in terms of Christian thinking adds a dimension of depth. Christians are citizens of two worlds, not just the present world of physical flesh. Christians hold that God's inclusive purpose for all mankind is back of moral requirements and that each individual is of infinite worth. Thus, an individual's fulfilling his highest destiny within the inclusive purpose of God becomes each man's divinely imposed obligation. And since society helps or hinders this, God's judgment is understood to be upon both individuals and society. Moreover, God's purpose and judgment are understood to extend beyond this life to include immortality.

We can state the inclusive perfectionist theory we have just described in the words of Professor Tsanoff as follows: "The highest value is the one manifesting the greatest expression and fulfillment of personality." (Radoslav A. Tsanoff, *Ethics,* pp. 116–117; Harper & Brothers, 1947.) Obviously, in pursuit of such a moral goal as this, the widest possible knowledge is required. So also is the strongest possible motivation required. This is especially true for the Christian in view of the fact that the fulfillment of a man's personality includes his becoming a child of God — an immortal. The apostle Paul expressed the idea that man can press on — as he himself was determined to do — toward the mark of the upward call. (Phil. 3:14.)

Two Kinds of Perfectionism Compared

But we must do more than merely state a definition of perfectionism, since two kinds of perfectionism have been held as ideal. The ideal can be stated as requiring in practice that chief emphasis be placed either on the individual or on the group.

Sharp conflict arises in consequence of the emphasis made. Indeed, the reason the world is gripped with fear that World War III may be about to shatter civilization at this present moment (as I write in mid-July, 1958) arises out of this conflict of ideals. On the one hand is a wholly social view of what ought to be in conduct; and on the other is the view that individuals, as such, must be our chief concern in morals. The latter is the view of our Western culture.

So also in individualistic perfectionism we assume that the highest good will be realized when individuals of a social order have both freedom and opportunity to develop themselves to the highest possible extent of their capabilities. In keeping with such an ideal, we in the United States insist upon free speech, free worship, free enterprise, and the like — for the individual. Yet this is not to the disregard of society. In such a scheme we consider that the inclusive social good will best be brought about as free men develop themselves in a social order — which means individuals developing themselves in relation to, and in co-operation with, other men similarly engaged.

Social perfectionism is set sharply over against this. As in the case of a communistic (or other) absolutism, it is assumed that individualism breaks down the social order. Individualism atomizes society, so to speak; society becomes an ineffective, conflicting mass of individuals who sacrifice the welfare of the whole for the personal good of each. And all seize the present gain at the expense of what may be a larger need later on.

Besides, this latter view contends that individuals are really nothing except a social order coming to individual awareness. What is the individual apart from the society and culture that produced him? Society provides the individual his language, his law, his science, his art, his religion — all of his culture. Thus, it is contended that the individual has no rights that society as a whole is bound to respect. The individual finds his fulfillment — which, of course, he must in any case — in the society that produced him. He must make society's objectives his objectives.

If we but follow through such reasoning as the above, we can find an answer to the questions we often raise about what communists mean when they use words like justice, right, freedom, democracy, and truth. With the ideal of society as the standard, their meaning flatly contradicts what we mean when we make use of the same terms. And it is pointless to say that a case cannot be made out for this way of looking at things. To say that in an absolutist state, such as Mussolini and Hitler sought to establish and such as is represented in present-day Russia and China, we simply have power-hungry, ruthless, enslaving dictatorship gone mad — this, too, is beside the point. Such systems use plausible arguments to justify their programs. They must in order to gain local and world support.

Such arguments are not hard to find. Individualism, such as a democracy like our country represents, is indeed wasteful. We mortgage the future in order to possess the present — as is evident in every bond issue for schools or roads. We do advocate the idea of economy for the public treasury; but at the same time we, as individual communities or special groups, try to get the largest possible amounts from that treasury. As indicated above, we must recognize the indebtedness of the individual to the group in which he lives. Certain psychologists have insisted that the individual is simply an eddy in the social current. While one might argue this point, it certainly would be mere waste of time to argue the independence of individuals in such matters as law, morals, or religion. In all such matters the individual is to a great extent a captive of the group.

Furthermore, we must allow the argument that individuals are socially motivated. We cannot achieve self-fulfillment by simply following individual biological urges. Here is a matter on which confusion sometimes arises. Popular statements say "obey that impulse" and "he serves society best who is most deeply and most intelligently concerned only with his own interest." Such statements seem to indicate that man is simply motivated by nature or by himself. But this is not the whole truth. It is quite true that man, being a biological organism, is motivated toward self as is any other biological organism. Men are driven by great biological hungers for the maintenance of life and its reproduction. So also the plant seeks food and water for maintenance and produces flowers and seed for reproduction. But it is also true that man cannot live alone. Life requires social relationships. Often this is true for life's maintenance and always it is true for reproduction. No man lives to himself alone.

Confusion as to the extent to which nature or society motivates the individual can be noted in another way. Nature has shut man fast within a sensory organism for all his experience, including the experience of satisfaction or self-fulfillment. We derive our consciousness of satisfaction from what we suppose other people think (or should think) of us or from how we suppose God regards us. Such facts are quite beyond dispute. And because of such facts it might seem easy to say we are children of nature and should, therefore, be content to let nature take its course. But we cannot in fact do that, for we are certainly no more children of nature than we are children of society. For while it is true that experience of all kinds (including the consciousness of self-fulfillment) must arise within the framework of the limited number of senses we have, the meaning of experiences must arise out of our sensory contact with objects — including other persons. Society will not allow us to express our urges when and how we please. We cannot completely command our sensory experiences from within. Society, also, impresses itself upon our senses from without.

With the above paragraphs we would attempt to keep clear the relationship of the individual to society. Also we recognize some validity to the argument that perfect individuals will be produced by a perfect social order. Persons are persons only in society. One psychologist used to insist strongly on this point in this way: if, conceivably, a man were something apart from the relationships he sustains as worker, citizen, parent, friend, husband, brother, and the like, it would be quite impossible to say what he was.

Nevertheless, while admitting that persons must live in society and that the kind of society they live in determines their development as individuals, still it remains true that persons create society. Persons living in society determine the aims and goals of society. Ethically, great differences arise out of the objectives aimed at by individual perfectionism as over against those of a wholly social perfectionism. A society aiming at individual perfection will seek to limit the functions of its social machinery where it is deemed necessary in order to safeguard the freedom requisite to individual development. A society wholly committed to social perfectionism would seek to accomplish the largest possible group ends in a process that would limit the freedom of individuals.

The Problem of Freedom Versus Security

Commitment of a society to the objectives of individual perfectionism creates a difficult problem in the public order. A line has to be drawn somewhere between what is essential for man as a social being and the freedom required for self-realization as a person. Some areas of personal freedom have to be given up for social welfare. Physical safety and security against disease and poverty require this. There can be no questioning of the necessity. But — the exact place where the line is to be drawn, that cannot be fixed definitely and finally. Ongoing life makes a once-for-all decision impossible. Changes are constantly occurring in the social, political, economic, and even the moral order. These facts are the chief cause of the perennial debates between groups whom we commonly call " conservatives " and " liberals." To sincere people who would like to see problems solved once for all, these debates are, no doubt, confusing or even amazing. But no real alternative exists to having such debates unless one could be either a complete anarchist (against all law) on the one hand or a convinced absolutist on the other.

As we consider moral ideals in the light of the nature of man as a person, neither of the above alternatives seems very real. The debates will continue. One thing stands clear: man must necessarily have both a sense of security within a social order *and* a sense of freedom. Some security is necessary as indicated. But, no matter how complete that security is, it can never be an end in itself. This is true from reasons also indicated: that *self*-motivated activity is the basic characteristic of all living things, i.e., freedom. Security is only a means, never an end. We can illustrate this by one of the most common ideas associated with immortality. At the same time we can indicate how closely associated with Christian thinking is the ethical view we have been discussing. Consider the common Christian concept of heaven. Heaven is thought of as a place where there is complete security. Heaven has been said to offer security from disease, death, poverty, ignorance, physical limitations, and the like. At the same time such security is for the purpose of free activity. Heaven is freedom to pursue the most worth-while activities endlessly.

Short of heaven, complete security and complete freedom seem impossible. Some freedom must be sacrificed for security. However, too much security is self-defeating. Doubtless President Eisenhower was thinking along such lines when he declared that where people are concerned he is a liberal, but where money is concerned, he is a conservative. That is to say, he was wrestling with this difficult problem of the public order: drawing a line between freedom and security. He saw the function of government as including efforts to find a way to make people secure, while at the same time free to exert themselves in a direction that seems to them desirable. Such reasoning reflects the ideal of individual perfectionism in our American life as the basic principle on which to base moral living. This ideal includes the Christian concept of the immortal character of the human soul.

CHRISTIAN MORALS AND SCIENTIFIC THINKING

Some further reasons in support of the foregoing view should not be overlooked. These reasons have to do with the understanding of persons and the world from the Christian viewpoint and from the viewpoint of modern science.

The Christian Idea of Individual Worth

One reason we contend for individual perfectionism as an ethical theory is the Christian idea of the unique and irreplaceable value of the individual person. Persons are not like machines or horses, whose value can be judged in terms of replacement cost. Persons are all different, and therefore cannot be replaced. They are, in a sense, permanent and indestructible. I have often said that every frustrated person could, if he only tried, give his discouraged ego a reassuring pat on the back. If one starts with the conviction that perfection is a quality in the power back of the universe, then considers himself a part of the universe (since he is obviously a part of it), he will come to see that the universe itself would be in some way short and incomplete if he were out of it.

If Christians are correct in saying that persons are real in the true sense of permanence, then the universe itself can have no higher aims than those of individual persons. If God had a reason for the creation of the world, that reason must have included persons as his most important objective.

In passing, we may remark that what we are here saying contains a lesson for those Christians who think of the church chiefly as an agent to bring about an ideal social order. Such thinking often fails to place a proper emphasis on the need for — and right to — conscious self-fulfillment in his own living to which an individual Christian is entitled. The church first of all embodies Christ's principle of abundant living in the ongoing experience of men and women as a fact of individual experience. The embodiment in Christians of abundant living then becomes the means by which God acts in and through his body — the church — to accomplish his purpose for the world. To think of the church chiefly as an agent for God's ultimate end may tend to make us consider individual, present Christians chiefly as a means to that end instead of first of all as ends in themselves. Such a way of thinking is like sacrificing the family in order to save society. Or, as the apostle Paul puts it, it is like preaching the gospel to others and becoming a castaway oneself. (I Cor. 9:27, KJV.)

Value Experience and the Complex Nature of Personality

An important scientific fact underscores Christian individual perfectionism as the basic moral ideal. This principle is that individuals must be the centers of value experience. Social values are nonexistent apart from the individuals who actually experience the values. All experience is personal and individual. Thus, all value — including the value of morals and religion — is reducible to what is capable of being experienced and accepted as valuable by individuals. Any sort of general values must be general only in the sense that they are (or can be) experienced by all the persons considered. Masses of persons, as masses, cannot experience values. It is persons, as persons, that are the sole center of value experience.

We must recognize, of course, that persons are not simple. A person is a very complex psychological organization. This has long been known. Augustine, for example, in his *Confessions* considered the nature of persons and spoke of the marvels of such facts as memory and forgetfulness. He said:

> When I remember memory, my memory itself is present to itself; but when I remember forgetfulness, then memory and forgetfulness are present together — forgetfulness which I remember, and memory by which I remember. But what is forgetfulness except absence of memory? How then can that be present to me to remember which when it is present means that I cannot remember? (F. J. Sheed, tr., *The Confessions of St. Augustine,* Books I–X, p. 185; Sheed & Ward, Inc., 1942.)

How indeed?

But in spite of the complexity of persons, we do know certain things very well. We know that each person possesses certain qualities or characteristics peculiarly his own. He is characterized also by knowledge or a degree of understanding. He is known by his social relationships or fellowship. He possesses ideals, which are his hopes and wishes. Personality is characterized in these ways, but it is more. It includes the organization of the various characterizations into a whole — an integrated, dynamic process. Personality is goal-seeking and goal-realizing. It is never-ending. One cannot write finis with regard to it, for it is never completed, always becoming. Indeed, one can say that if personality is real, it must be immortal, for only that which is permanent is real in a true sense. Thus it is that what we have said about the Christian dimension of depth is also in keeping with what we are now saying about the concept of value as being real.

Personality, as thus understood scientifically, is the selfhood whose realization we are accepting as the basic end to be sought in moral conduct. Nevertheless, as previously indicated, this understanding of self or personality does not overlook society. Indeed, the self can realize the highest and best only in a society of selves seeking similar personal and social ends. Self-defeat results when a person tries to live selfishly. Scientific inquiry into the nature of selfhood offers abundant evidence of this fact. In this we agree, and further add that moral failure also results from living for self alone, neglecting the social nature of oneself. Thus, science justifies the Biblical statement that no man lives to himself alone (Rom. 14:7).

Understood in this way, selfhood cannot be achieved within the brief limits of this life. This should be easy to see. The present life cannot even explore, to say nothing of realizing, the possibilities of persons. What earnest student, for example, has not wished for a length of years equal to many lifetimes in order to explore the fields of interest he sees? And this is to say nothing of realizing all the possibilities of persons as those possibilities exist beyond the mind of man in the mind of God — or the possibilities within the gift of God. What a thrilling prospect is the hope of an eternal progression of persons in truth, beauty, and goodness!

Thus, a consideration of a person or a self leads us to this Christian conclusion: mind, God, immortality. Mind is the real with which all thought and all meaning in every field must start. One can say that mind is the real agent of all effort and abandon the quest there; or one can say as the Christian does that the source of mind is God. This latter is a better resting place. Not only does it end in an embodiment of the qualities in persons that we call mind but also that which in nature we call the reign of law and the principle of growth, cohesion, and concretion. The only really satisfactory explanation of mind is God. And immortality is required because personal mind is a permanent fact, a characteristic of the universe.

CHAPTER

III

Influences on Moral Judgments

THE MORAL IDEAL is more easily stated than lived up to. The very nature of any ideal such as we have discussed is to serve as an eventual standard by which to judge moral conduct. But the fact is that our moral judgments are almost always on-the-spot judgments instead of long-range judgments. Many immediate considerations influence our judgments of conduct and often warp them out of line with a long-range view. Thus it is much easier to know what the long-range ideal should be than it is to do that which conforms to it in an immediate situation. The purpose in this chapter is to discuss briefly some of the influences that enter into our on-the-spot judgments. Frequently these influences, if ignored or misunderstood, can confuse us and lead us astray from pressing on toward our ideal.

CONFLICTING INTERESTS

One of the most obvious facts about our social experience is that interests conflict. We often feel a sense of duty (or obligation) in situations where we find it impossible to act in such a way that we meet the rival claims being made upon us by our various interests. One may, for example, feel a duty to his work and at the same time feel a duty to his home and family that would require him to neglect his work. Or one may feel a sense of responsibility to aid an important civic or humanitarian cause when doing so interferes with his obligation to his profession or his family. Nobody can expect to escape such conflicts. But obviously it ought to be possible for us to make such an appraisal of ourselves and of our situations as will enable us to live at peace with ourselves and to learn, as did the apostle Paul, to be content in our state, whatever the circumstances may be (Phil. 4:11). We need, therefore, to see what people usually consider right in cases of conflicting interests. Then we shall need to see how we can be sure of what is right. The result of this will be a recognition of what our duty is in the immediate situation.

When faced with conflicting interests, we are likely to feel, and often be guided by, certain preferences that seem to us at the time to be good and right. A number of considerations that commonly influence people in their actions were so well stated by Prof. Frank Chapman Sharp, in his great book *Ethics* (ch. 3, pp. 37–51; Century Company, 1928), that we certainly cannot do better than follow his list. Sharp discussed what he labeled the primacy of the greater good, the more striking good, the good of the nearer, and the good of the more excellent. It will not be necessary to follow his analysis in detail here. It will be helpful to consider briefly each of these influences upon our moral judgments before going on to discuss the nature and influence of conscience and the meaning of duty. Our purpose is not to pronounce these influences good or bad but simply to record them as real. Being thus put on guard, we may not fall into unsound moral decisions where these influences are present.

The Primacy of the Greater Good

Moral action is always action motivated by the feeling that something ought to be done because it is better than something else. In practice, this feeling guides toward choosing a particular course of action as better than its alternative because it seems likely to bring about better results. Such a choice may be made even though it is recognized that the alternative, considered by itself, may be a moral obligation also. The influence on moral choice that is at work here can be called the primacy of the greater good.

For example, most people — although not all — would justify the stealing of a loaf of bread by a man if that were his only way to escape starvation. They would not mean by this that stealing is right. They would mean only that such a general principle as "Thou shalt not steal" has to be interpreted for practical purposes in the light of available choices. In this instance, the sustaining of life would seem to be the greater good.

So also, if one must lie to save a life, or if a statesman must dissemble and mislead regarding the facts in order to prevent a war, most people would justify following such a course since it is calculated, as they see it, to bring about the greatest good under the circumstances. It is beside the point to say that in such case a lie is not a lie. That would involve us in the question of what a lie is — whether lying implies a mere misstatement of facts or instead the violation of a moral obligation regardless of the facts as mere facts. The point here is that people generally approve that action from among the available alternatives which seems calculated to result in the greatest good.

The Primacy of the More Striking Good

This influence is stated by Sharp as follows: "The more vividly a good is realized, the higher do we rate its claims" (p. 41). Consider, for example, the case of Capt. Robert F. Scott, of the British Navy, who reached the South Pole on January 18, 1912. He and his companions were caught in a violent blizzard on the way back to base camp. Captain Scott realized that he, personally, could not make it back, but he thought his companions might if they abandoned him. But they would not do that. So while they were in their sleeping bags, Captain Scott crept out into the snow to die in the polar cold. As it turned out, it was a fruitless sacrifice, for his companions did not make it back to base either. Nevertheless, when the diary recounting what happened was found, *all* were acclaimed heroes and held in highest honor. And this in spite of the fact that the pole had been reached before Scott's party had reached it. Both the selfless devotion of Scott's companions and the heroic self-sacrifice of Scott — these deeds, even though they proved unavailing, were strikingly good deeds regardless of what they brought about in the way of results. Moreover, it can be pointed out that giving oneself for others is a Christian virtue as well as sometimes being a striking good.

Most people are influenced in their moral judgments by the striking character of a given act or course of action. This is the primacy of the more striking good. Such an influence as this, it should be noted, may lead one toward judging a quality exhibited by a person when he imagines he is judging the quality of an act.

National patriotism provides a good illustration of an influence of this sort. As I write this in the summer of 1958 the political situation in the Near East is one of confusion; small nations are undergoing revolution or threat of revolution. Suppose in this situation that it were possible for these nations to be absorbed completely by Russia or by another power? Suppose that by doing this these small nations would lose their national identity but otherwise would not suffer at all. Would it then be morally right for them to yield to such a political change, forgetful of their own national hopes and aspirations? No doubt few persons could be found to agree that such a course of action would necessarily be morally right. The reasoning would seem to be that nationalism as such is a striking good that we tend to approve without questioning the results flowing out of it. It seems obvious that patriotism is good; law and government must have public support if mankind is to escape anarchy.

At the same time it has to be admitted that nationalism is responsible for many problems in today's world where both commerce and defense have to be thought of in world terms. In terms of moral judgments we must be on our guard in such matters. As patriots we are apt to see nationalism as a striking good that elicits a favorable ethical judgment, especially if such judgment relates to matters of our own national defense and sovereignty. But if we are Christians as well as patriots, we must be careful. While completely justifying our own patriotic devotion, we may condemn other nations — especially weaker nations —

whose citizens are equally committed to their own national hopes and ideals, which may be at variance with our own. We have to remember that we cannot divorce patriotic judgments from moral judgments. Appeals for the support of national honor and national hopes must be justified at last on moral grounds.

The Primacy of the Good of the Nearer

The influence suggested by the good of the nearer is simply this: we are likely to judge those most closely related to us as more deserving of good than those far away. This fact is so common as to need no supporting illustration or attempts at proof. If a son of the governor were guilty of a capital crime, we would probably expect the executive to pardon him and then to resign immediately afterward. More frequent is the recognition by a judge that it is his duty to disqualify himself in a case before the court over which he presides in which members of his family have some special interest. Were he to preside, his judgment would be influenced by the good of those persons of nearer kinship. We simply must recognize that the primacy of the good of the nearer is a characteristic of our judgments.

Recognition of this influence on moral judgments is often involved in troublesome questions for Christians. Many Christians are troubled at the point of seeking to conform to Jesus' principle of the brotherhood of all mankind. They acknowledge the principle but constantly find in practice that they actually love their own people better than they love others. Here again the facts of the situation are obvious and require no supporting evidence. But what should be remembered is this: the feeling of nearness to persons (which we use in connection with the good of the nearer) arises out of the fact of being near. In other words, the sense of close relationship grows out of the fact of being closely related. We may illustrate by saying that as a good citizen one is bound up with the whole town, city, state, and nation; but in the exercise of one's citizenship he is more closely related to, and consequently more aware of, his next-door neighbor than he is of a man living on the other side of town or across the nation whom he does not personally know. Moreover, one must exercise his citizenship *where he lives.* He cannot neglect citizenship with regard to his immediate neighbor and hope to become a good citizen of the larger community or the world. Similarly, people cannot neglect their own homes in particular and expect to improve society.

Christians who are disturbed because they cannot love a hungry child on the other side of the world as much as they love their own children should acknowledge that the reason they do not is because they cannot. And they should recognize also that they cannot be expected so to love. The feeling of nearness can only accompany some kind of experience capable of giving rise to it. The science of psychology (which is our guide in matters of this kind) knows of no such thing as an uncaused feeling, just as the science of physics knows of no such thing as an uncaused result. Unless, or until, a Christian has an experience capable of giving rise to love for a hungry child on the other side of the world, he will probably continue to love his own child more.

But at the same time, while Christians cannot feel toward everybody exactly alike, they can wish all mankind well. They can wish all men peace, justice, security, freedom from poverty and disease; they can wish all men an opportunity to active self-fulfillment. This is what the Christian ideal of the brotherhood of all men means. It does not mean that we should set ourselves the impossible task of coming to feel toward everybody's children as deeply as we feel for our own, since this would involve having with everybody's children the intimate experiences we share with our own. But what we must guard against is the other extreme: allowing the primacy of the good of the nearer to blind us to the rights and needs of those whom we could, and should, help. The impossibility of feeling near to everybody does not absolve the Christian from the ideal of brotherhood as we have stated it above. As there is opportunity to promote the self-fulfillment of others, this should be done. The basis of the action is the wish — the desire — for the ideal of brotherhood, not the already experienced feeling of love. If those earnest Christians who are deeply troubled about problems of race equality could be brought to see that brotherhood among the races as a goal for Christians does not imply the extension of a feeling of nearness and intimacy to everybody in the world, they would doubtless find color and class prejudices easier to dismiss. Nobody can feel intimate acquaintance or intimate emotional regard for persons in the absence of intimate social contact.

Here in our discussion is something that theologians sometimes try to help us understand by reminding us of the differing meanings of certain Greek words used in the New Testament which are intended to point out what Christian love is. But we need not be theologians in order to understand the simple psychological principle that controls us. The principle is that feelings are caused, and in order to have feelings we must be in situations that can give rise to them. The feeling of nearness arises, as we have already said, out of the fact of nearness. Likewise, the feeling of parenthood arises out of the fact of being a parent; the feeling of being a farmer arises out of the activities of farming; the feeling of being a doctor or a lawyer arises out of the experiences of these professions. Just so, this principle applies to the whole circle of relationships of the Christian—both when he judges what is right and when he is functioning morally as a citizen.

The Primacy of the Good of the More Excellent

Here is a principle which we not infrequently employ in moral judgments. If we are asked to justify the conduct of a person who has attained excellence in some field of endeavor, we may approve on the ground that the excellent deserve more reward than others and that the reward in turn stimulates further excellence. To argue that moral judgments can be thus justified is not the purpose here, as we have already indicated. But it is necessary for us to be aware of the influence that is brought to bear on our moral judgments because of the presence of excellence in some area other than morals.

Some years ago a newspaper contained an editorial dealing with the moral problem created when a prisoner was given a furlough from prison in order to journey to another state where a musical production he had composed was to be given a special rendition. The fact that this man had produced the music and had been given a furlough to go hear its rendition resulted in some agitation from some persons to obtain a pardon for the man. Here was a good case of the influence of this principle: the primacy of the good of the excellent. In this case the editor simply raised the question, "Should this man be pardoned?" He declined to answer editorially, saying that he was very glad he was not required to do so.

Troublesome situations frequently arise in day-to-day activities because of this influence. School boys may be guilty of cheating in a class where they dislike the teacher, when they do not cheat in the class of a teacher of whom they approve. A judge in a traffic court may dismiss a fine for a fellow officer that he would not dismiss for a mere citizen. But worse than these instances, a man who supposes himself to be excellent in one way may come to expect preferred treatment in some way or another not related to his excellence. This we are likely to call "special privilege" when we condemn others who benefit by it. At the same time we may easily fail to recognize when we ourselves receive special treatment.

CONSCIENCE

The fact of conscience is a guide in the correctness of a moral judgment. It is often referred to and used. But it should be obvious from the foregoing discussion that such influences as mentioned are brought to bear in the formation of what our consciences tell us we ought to do. This brings us to the basic question regarding conscience: Can we follow our consciences? If a man conscientiously does what he does, is what he does therefore right? People often say, "My conscience doesn't condemn me, so I know

I am doing right." Must we agree? To a consideration of how such questions are to be answered we now turn.

Conscientiousness

Perhaps of more practical consequence than defining conscience at this point is a consideration of conscientiousness. By conscientiousness we mean acting according to conscience. Obviously, it is a better thing for persons to act conscientiously than for them to act otherwise, or to act from motives that are recognized as evil. Conscientiousness guarantees that such moral insights as we possess will not be prostituted to evil ends.

But a certain kind of conscientiousness disturbs most of us and may become one of the real annoyances of life if we are subjected to it constantly. I refer to that conscientiousness that insists on magnifying little things and insists on details that cannot matter much. Many years of experience with college students have taught me that this is not infrequently a problem area of experience. A student finds a five-cent pencil and troubles himself about theft if he doesn't try to find the owner or at least place it with the Lost and Found. Another student reported always driving his car to a parking meter with no time registered on it in order not to cheat the city, since the city expected some return for every car parked. When that particular action was called to my attention, I replied that I often did something of the kind except that I reversed the process, looking for a meter with time remaining! Again an illustration comes to mind out of my experiences when lecturing on the evils of gambling. Sometimes I have been asked how I regarded matching pennies to see who gets an extra available dessert at the dining hall. The question always is, "Isn't that gambling?" Of course the answer is "yes." However, the important thing is not approached by the wording of the question. Of course, one must recognize the principle that gambling is evil and that a particular instance is, or is not, consistent with the principle. But beyond this, one must decide if conformity to the principle in a particular situation is of much real consequence. If one chooses to act contrary to the principle on the ground that nothing of consequence is involved in a particular case, he avoids throwing dust in his own eyes and so creating moral confusion. Confusion would result if he tried to argue that matching pennies is not really gambling.

Similarly, I have heard it argued that it was wrong to thank one's hostess for a party that turned out to be a boresome evening. The wrong involved was a lie, or at least prevarication. I have known conscientious persons who tried to rationalize the situation so as to be convinced that lying was not involved; others who simply assumed that lying was involved and justified a discourteous remark to the hostess on the ground that they must tell the truth to her. But again, as in the case of gambling above, the important thing is recognizing the principle of truthfulness as a valid principle and then applying the principle in the light of what is reasonable in the circumstances.

The overly conscientious person often becomes involved in something much worse than just indicated. Such a person may become a talebearer on the ground that the truth ought to be told. He may say to you, "I think you ought to know that Mrs. S. said some nasty things about you." He then proceeds to tell you what the nasty things were, even when no possible good could come out of the telling. In fact, things could be truly said about any one of us that could benefit nobody in the telling. Doubtless most of us could make confessions regarding the past that might influence the opinion friends or family hold of us. But if they are truly past and are not now indicators of our true character, and if only harm could come in the telling, they should be forgotten, not repeated.

Conscientiousness is important and desirable as we have indicated. But confusion in moral judgment often arises from conscientiousness which insists on unvarying application of important moral principles to trifling details. Such conscientiousness falls into the legalism Jesus sought to avoid when he declared that the Sabbath was made for man, not man for the observance of the law of the Sabbath (Mark 2:23–28).

The Judgments of Conscience

What then is conscience? And to what extent can we depend on conscience as a guide toward right living? The former of these two questions has been answered in contrasting ways. The theological answer contends that conscience is the voice of God within us. A philosophical empiricist answers that conscience is the voice of experience and training. If we try to follow either of these answers as a sure guide, we will land in difficulties from which it will be impossible to extricate ourselves. Here Prof. Radoslav A. Tsanoff helps us again with these suggestions:

> Whether resisting the strong incursion of evil or judging between contending obligations, conscience involves the emergence of one or another character. . . . Moral character is not abstractly permanent; it is ever in the process of self-molding. . . . Conscience is the voice of a man's fuller self, the man that he may yet be. (P. 153.)

Conscience then can be thought of as the whole man—the man that is and the man that is to be—passing judgment on acts. Some ethical writers dismiss the matter by calling conscience the whole mind passing judgment on volitions. (See Sharp, p. 113.)

From this reasoning it becomes apparent that what conscience tells us to do may not be infallibly right. Ignorance may exist; so may errors in judgment. Still, we must be guided in present situations by conscience. There is no other way, since our moral reasoning at any moment includes all our experience and the knowledge so far obtained from it. This is consistent with what was said in Chapter I concerning the gaining of knowledge from the voice of God.

Also consistent with what has been said about moral growth, acting conscientiously in the light of our experience really requires a growing, changing conscience as new experience and better understanding enable us to see better ways. The Christian's conscience should grow in the direction of a constantly wider understanding and appreciation of the principles of good. Thus, I have often said that the Christian whose conscience has not changed about anything as he has grown older should take no satisfaction from that fact. Instead he ought to be alarmed by it, for he has missed the meaning of living by the spirit of the law instead of by its letter. He has failed to grow in grace.

DUTY

We are now able to talk about our duty. Duty is defined in terms of active obligation — something to do, to pay, to accomplish. But one interesting thing about duty is that just what should be done varies with the circumstances. The old saying, "Circumstances alter cases," has meaning when duty is being considered. Duty must always be considered in something less than an absolute, unvarying sense. We discuss duty, therefore, in general terms, leaving the individual to determine his duty in the circumstances and to apply the principles as he sees his duty.

This fact — that individuals must apply principles according to circumstances — is one compelling reason why we are considering such matters as we have in this chapter. Snap judgments are often misleading, as we have stated; but at the same time, it also remains true that all our active judgments have to be on-the-spot judgments, so to speak. Therefore, we must give serious consideration to principles that ought to guide us in order that the application may be at once clear in immediate circumstances.

Long experience with students has established my conviction that people often worry about what they ought to do, or ought to have done, when such questions need not trouble them at all. Such worry occurs because people fail to see clearly that the Christian ideal for personal conduct is being guided by principles — the spirit, instead of the letter, of the law. Such principles exist and are clear enough when we give attention to them. With such attention, their application in the circumstances where we find ourselves is also likely to be instantly clear.

Consider, for example, in the present context so-called "conflicting duty." The principle here is that duties cannot, in fact, conflict. This means that if I determine that my duty requires one course of action, making impossible a conflicting course, then the conflicting course cannot be my duty. There the matter ends. Regret for the existence of the seeming conflict changes nothing.

In this connection, it is also clear that duty cannot require the impossible. Good people sometimes seem to think that their actions should conform to an ideal, such as the ideal of truth or peace or personal rights, regardless of whether or not the circumstances make such ideal actions possible. I suppose this is one reason why good people often deplore politics and hold politicians in contempt, in spite of obvious dependence of our public ideals on politics and politicians. Politics is commonly spoken of as "the science of the possible." Those who represent us in politics frequently appear to make compromises in areas where it seems to us that only one right way exists. The criticism of many good people frequently overlooks the fact that the ideal which we cherish cannot be reached; achievement of it is not possible. The ideal is a flying goal. It provides us guidance in a proper direction, not a stopping place. It helps us to choose the best from among our live options. And we cannot refuse to choose. Living is choosing — acting — not merely sitting in judgment on actions! Furthermore, we cannot perform every good, because performing one means leaving another unperformed. Thus we say that moral living — doing one's duty without constant personal recrimination — is living in the light of the ideal, not constantly achieving the ideal.

Qualifications Concerning Duty

One qualification concerning duty is raised by asking, "What is the good?" When we discuss duty we are concerned with what we ought to do in order to bring good about. But, of course, if we are to bring about good, we must have some knowledge of what good is. What then do you mean by good? Do you mean the will of God is good? Is it conceivable that his will should be different from the genuine welfare of men?

Arguments arising over such questions as these are usually due to our tendency to overlook one important fact, namely, that our only way to characterize God or to think of his will is in terms of our own human values. We cannot think of God's will as requiring hate or the performance of those acts which we regard as ultimately destructive of human values such as love, goodness, beauty, truth, justice, and the like. Good turns out to be, after all, what people think of as good. Thus, the will of God and the welfare of men turn out to be the same thing in the long run. This remains true in spite of the fact that we can imagine God's justice as requiring man's punishment under certain circumstances.

Such considerations will qualify our concept of duty. The concept of duty we hold should be that which, so far as we can see, will bring about the greatest human good possible in the circumstances. This good may be one's own good, if that is greater, because the individual is always a part of the whole. But here we must be on guard. One is not usually qualified to judge that his own good is the greatest good. This is true because of such influences on one's judgment as were discussed in the opening pages of this chapter. Thus one might be helped in determining his duty—if time and circumstances permit—to seek the opinion of some less partial persons. Such advice may indicate that one should perhaps sacrifice some of his personal good in the interests of others. Or one's own first judgment might be confirmed.

In any event, there is one qualification concerning the extent to which one must sacrifice his own interests and preferences for the good of others. Since the individual is always a part of the whole in any moral situation and since the individual is always an end as well as a means to the fulfillment of God's total purpose, he can feel free in asserting his right to the use of such resources as he may possess toward his own self-development. At the same time, one must recognize that he must be on guard against self-aggrandizement as such. As an instance of properly using one's resources, I may have a perfect right to spend money for an education or other cultural advancement when that same money might also have been spent on food and shelter for the poor. In such cases, we recognize ourselves as ends of God's purpose rather than as means only.

While what is said here is intended to be suggestive rather than exhaustive, even such a short discussion requires one further consideration concerning duty. Such a consideration can serve both to bring this chapter to a close and to introduce the next topic, the family — which is perhaps the most important of these studies. That consideration is this: some duties, once assumed, cannot be put aside on account of other later claims that may appear on the surface to have greater weight. Marriage and family claims are of this sort. That one has a duty to his work, to his profession, to the fulfillment of his capabilities as an artist or musician — such duties can be granted readily; but such duty cannot absolve one from his responsibilities to his wife and family. Family duties are sometimes called "perfectly binding obligations" because once they exist their undeniable claims cannot be fulfilled by any other course of action. Celibate Christian groups provide us a valuable reminder at this point by warning us against multiplication of perfectly binding obligations. If a man's particular vocation has a right to be considered a perfectly binding obligation, he does not then have the right to assume the obligations of home and family, since by their nature they too are perfectly binding obligations, which would eventually lead to a conflict of obligations. (Further reference will be made to such obligations in the chapters that follow.)

The obligation to family is, then, a perfect moral obligation. If the family is the ultimate social unit — and God has set nature's seal upon it by assigning to it the creative function — then it is impossible for any other functions in society to take precedence over family obligations, once they exist. In view of this fact, it is not strange that Jesus varied his customary practice of giving us only guiding principles instead of laws. In speaking of obligation to family, his words are more than guidance. He said:

> Have you not read that he who made them from the beginning made them male and female, and said, "For this reason a man shall leave his father and mother and be joined to his wife, and the two shall become one"? So they are no longer two but one. What therefore God has joined together, let no man put asunder. (Matt. 19:4–6.)

CHAPTER IV

The Family

FROM THE VERY FIRST we have stressed that moral requirements are of such immediate and practical significance that we cannot wait for unanimous theological agreement among Christians before adopting a moral ideal. We then discussed the very minimum of ethical theory in order to explain our ideal of individual perfectionism as a moral theory useful in practical Christian living. We have just concluded an examination of certain common terms and experiences of moral judgment to the extent necessary to avoid confusion in our day-to-day judgments. In terms of most books dealing with morals and ethics, we have been dealing with "theory." Yet the reader cannot help being aware from our illustrations that our intent has been practical, not theological or philosophical (although the theological and philosophical viewpoint from which we are writing could be defended at great length).

The remainder of these studies will deal with specific areas of human relations — practical daily situations — in which moral judgments are significant for the Christian. What we have written concerning the ideal of perfecting the individual — as he lives in society — will be assumed even if not specifically named. The thoughtful reader will see our ideal and the "theory" behind and beyond the considerations in the chapters that follow. We shall give attention now to that topic which, as we stated briefly in the preceding chapter, we consider to be one of great importance: the family.

THE HOME AND HAPPINESS

The family is regarded by mankind as offering life's highest possibilities of well-being, with resulting happiness. Particularly in our Western culture, we think of the family (and/or home) as providing that set of human relationships wherein the highest ideals of human welfare must be embodied if we expect to experience the best that is humanly possible for us. And the Christian observes this striking fact: when inspired writers were seeking for a word that would adequately describe ultimate reality, the word which came to them was one from the family relationship. *Father* was taken as the best description of God. So also, when they were trying to conceive of a place good enough in which to spend eternity, the idea of heaven as *home* was revealed to them. Nothing else but home could be good enough. Examples are numerous of the ideal way in which these words were used. The psalmist uses both words in successive verses:

> A father of the fatherless, and a judge of the widows,
> Is God in his holy habitation.
> God setteth the solitary in families. (Ps. 68:5–6, KJV.)

> Father of the fatherless and protector of widows
> is God in his holy habitation.
> God gives the desolate a home to dwell in. (RSV.)

The Family Ideal

In a sadly confused society such as ours, the persistence of the family ideal is an amazing fact — in spite of all that seems calculated to uproot this ideal. Think, for example, of the appalling divorce rate among us; of the loudmouthed quarreling between husband and wife that provides a stock-in-trade cartoon subject; of the glamorization of physical sex in movies and on television until romance seems destined to be stripped of all poetry, music, and flowers — marriage left to stand as stark biology or "chemical reaction." Still, in spite of everything, the family ideal persists! Men and women want good homes. They dream about them, work for them, and long to fashion and live in them. There, if anywhere, they expect to find fulfillment and the happiness that attends fulfillment in life.

The persistence of the ideal of home in spite of counterinfluences is noteworthy. But other important facts also suggest themselves when we think seriously about the home as our greatest personal concern. One such fact is this: in home and family relationships success or failure, happiness or sorrow are largely in the hands of those directly involved. If marriages are unhappy, those suffer most who make them so. Here the old saying, "Chickens come home to roost," is literally true. To be sure, other factors may interfere with the success of home and family — in-laws, "predatory" husbands and wives or other outsiders, accidents, diseases, and the inevitable stresses and frustrations of life. But while such factors may interfere, the fact remains that the biggest primary cause of success or failure in family life is the direct responsibility of those in the home for their actions. So, where a change is needed to improve the family ideal, the essential change must be a change in — or within — the persons directly involved.

The Place of Sex

Another factor not to be ignored in the happiness of home life is the fact of sex. We have just deplored the reduction of romance to sex as sex; but the fact of sex cannot be ignored without disastrous results for home and family. One ethical writer reminds us of the centrality of sex in common moral thinking by saying that in most minds "the terms moral and immoral, morality and immorality, are often identified exclusively with the special field of morals connected with the life of the sexes" (Wilbur Marshall Urban, *Fundamentals of Ethics: An Introduction to Moral Philosophy,* p. 287; Henry Holt & Co., Inc., 1930). It would be complete folly to ignore the fact of sex and its centrality in that area of morality which we are now discussing. Our purpose here does not include consideration of intimate questions concerning sex relations — questions that can be better left to physicians and counselors. Some general facts about the place of sex must not, however, be overlooked.

Sex is one of life's strongest instinctive urges. The psychiatrist would perhaps call it in its inclusive sense "*eros.*" So masterful is the mating disposition and so inclusive a guide is it to total social relations that certain psychologists have been disposed to attribute everything social to this urge ultimately. Curiously, people frequently speak of matters relating to sex as habits, when the fact is that such matters involve a fundamental human drive, a drive strongly suggestive of the hunger drive in its urgency. Nobody speaks of eating as if it were due to the formation of a habit of eating. Likewise, nobody should think of the exercise of sex as mere acts dictated by habits. True, there are sex practices that may become habitual, just as there are eating habits; but the drive itself is not due to habit. Instead, sex should be thought of as a basic part of human nature.

This basic activity in human nature must be understood in its proper perspective. To think of this disposition of human beings solely in terms of physical gratification (as some would do) is to depersonalize man — to project life on the social level of the barnyard. Rather, in sex we have something in the presence of which we properly marvel; we stand in awe. What we have here is not only a physical hunger but also our basic social force as well. Out of this force comes love, home, friendship, devotion, and self-sacrifice in the line of duty to society and even to God. We have previously said that we need no theological discriminations among the meanings of words in an ancient language in order to understand how the feeling of love arises. Love arises as meaning out of social experience. Back of such meaning is the urge to fulfillment of life; and such fulfillment includes, but is by no means confined to, the creative act by which new persons come into being. The place of sex will not be degraded when we keep in mind the importance of persons and of their individual fulfillment in cooperation with other persons and with the forces of the natural world that God created.

I have always been interested in the living, growing things that everywhere surround us. I have often marveled at the devices of nature by means of which life is sustained and perpetuated. What wonderful co-operative forces are brought into play to the end of life's fulfillment! And such co-operative forces are but variations on the theme of love — love, which is the cohesive power back of all living things.

Here it should be remembered that reproduction is not the only end in life. Love motivates the creative act as a part of life's fulfillment, but love motivates activity toward fulfillment in other ways also. In nature, a flower is no less an end or fulfillment when it produces its beauty of color as beauty itself than when its color attracts an insect to perform the act of pollenization. At the human level, the urge to life's fulfillment is no less furthered when one paints a picture for the love of beauty, or performs acts of self-sacrifice for love of human service, than when one is motivated to perform the creative act. The force back of all living things urging reproduction and the cohesive force by which all things consist as beauty and truth — this is one and the same force. The affinity of growing things for light, air, and moisture; the color and fragrance of flowers that invite insects to perform their pollenizing function; the color and taste of fruit and seed that invite living creatures not only to eat but also to plant; the social cohesion that is so surely a part of the nature of things that mankind must live together co-operatively or perish — all these are evidences of that characteristic of the universe which is the basic fact behind love, marriage, and home.

The place of sex in human life is central, but it is far from tawdry.

THE FAMILY AS WE KNOW IT

What we have been saying thus far has held the home and family life up as an ideal in human relations. In addition to what has already been said, we should observe some of the obvious ways in which the family contributes to individual self-fulfillment in the context of God's plan for his world.

A Link in the Chain of Being

The most important single fact about the family has already been suggested: family relationships arise out of the biological and social plan of life survival. The disposition of the creature to reproduce and to care for offspring gives rise to family relationships. This disposition likewise becomes a link in the chain of being (existence) which cannot be broken without destroying the whole scheme of the universe. The creature here participates in God's most important creative work. Here men and women become creators along with God. They are the creators, not of life alone but also of personality; and personality, as far as we can see, is God's aim in creating the universe.

This importance of personality in God's purpose has been stated before. It must be so. Living persons are what make the world of values real; and the presence of values causes one thing to be better than another, thus producing cosmos instead of chaos. This dependence of the universe (cosmos) on values, and of values on living beings, has been steadily implied in all we have said and should never be forgotten. The supposed reality and possibility of values — of good — is the basic assumption of morals.

All good that we suppose is possible must become actual (if indeed it ever becomes real) in the experience of persons. This is true even if we think of divine love as the ultimate or unconditioned good. If divine love is to have meaning in reality, our cue to the meaning of that love must be found by us in the human love experience. So also if we are to have any suggestion of the meaning of the divine order of truth, beauty, or justice, our understanding must arise out of human experience of truth, beauty, and justice. Words themselves, like love, truth, order, or law, are mere symbols without meaning until experience provides it. So the world of value, as well as life itself, depends upon that disposition in persons to reproduce and care for offspring. Family relationships arise out of this disposition; personality is fulfilled out of the family relationships; and the whole scheme of existence is continued. The very chain of being is thus dependent on that urge in humans which also produces the family.

A Plan for Division of Labor

Another contribution that the family makes toward fulfillment is perhaps more easily seen than that of which we have just been writing. The family provides a practical plan for co-operative division of labor between the sexes. Students studying the history of marriage point out that the family emerged, in part, as an economic unit. As the family developed, it was adapted to the practical needs for various kinds of co-operative effort. Man's needs as a living person demand co-operative effort. This is emphasized by the fact of a long period of helpless infancy and the need for assistance throughout life in obtaining food and shelter. So the family contributes to fulfillment of these needs.

This same contribution is evident in another perhaps larger way. For safety, men need to live in groups larger than families if families themselves are to survive. This driving social urge, while providing co-operative safety, invariably sets men in competition with their fellows. By comparison and contrast with other persons in the larger group, individuals recognize themselves as persons. But hazards, as well as benefits, also arise out of such competition as one considers his social status in comparison to others. The family grouping to which one may repair provides one with a secure social status within a small group wherein competition is largely replaced by co-operation.

A Background for Religious Feeling

The importance of the family is underscored by a contribution that it makes in an area of a person's fulfillment more closely related to his inner feelings. The experience of living in a family provides a person with a background for understanding the meaning of religion as a conscious experience. Basically, the religious feeling, as such, is a feeling of rapport—community. The real object of the religious quest is to reach a state of being in which one feels in harmony of thought and purpose with the Ultimate Reality. The religious person experiences this feeling in terms of a feeling of forgiveness or a feeling of acceptance. But here again, as with the experiencing of divine love a few paragraphs above, the meaning of rapport or the feeling of forgiveness must first of all arise out of experience on the human level. The family provides mankind with the nearest approach to conditions under which such a feeling of unity is possible. The family thus provides life's best opportunity for the individual to experience the meaning of rapport as rapport with God might be experienced.

A sound psychological principle was stated by the psalmist when he declared that God sets the solitary in families. Generally speaking, our relations with men leave us with a feeling short of full rapport. As we have said, we are in competition with them as well as in co-operation. Their purposes are not wholly our purposes; they do not see us as we see ourselves. But in the family the feeling is different. Hopes, successes, and failures are all common in a large degree. In the best of families a feeling of complete community arises where no hidden secrets mar the sense of rapport. Families are inescapably bound together in a common life. Psychologically then, if one is to be able to judge how acceptance before God feels — how it feels to be bound in a common life with him — the family relationship provides an area of human experience whereby this kind of feeling can be experienced and known.

A husband and wife by the fireside — he with his newspaper and she with her knitting and dreams — may be completely absorbed, each in his own employment so far as conscious awareness goes. Still, they may be so closely bound together in that unity which is true marriage that this fact becomes the bond that explains the sense of well-being and content that they experience. (This point should be remembered when we come to Chapter VI. The rupture of this bond — this rapport — while persons are still bound together in a common life makes marriages intolerable sometimes and produces divorce.) This experience and feeling of rapport emphasizes the importance of the family from the religious point of view. We have mentioned that men and women act with God to create living persons. But here is a religious reason for the importance of the family which goes beyond the creative function: the family provides a set of relationships out of which comes an understanding of what fellowship with God means. The basic urge that underlies the family has these deeper meanings than simple reproduction of the race. Certainly no one with an understanding of these deeper meanings should wonder at the fact that marriage rites have everywhere been accompanied by religious sanctions.

SOCIAL FACTORS AFFECTING THE FAMILY

Having considered the family ideal and the importance of the family in the fulfillment of life for the individual, we must also be aware of certain social factors that affect the achievement of that fulfillment. Some of these factors are changes that have taken place in our society within the past generation or two. Others are ways in which society has looked at family life for a longer time. As in some previous sections, our purpose is not to say that these conditions are right or wrong but rather to point out that ignorance or disregard for these factors may well interfere with one's moral judgments with regard to family relationships.

Technological and Economic Changes

Sweeping social changes during the past generation have had inevitable effects on the family. Among such changes, those of a technological and economic sort have been important for the family. The family — largely rural — used to be relatively independent and self-sufficient, but now families — largely urban — are very much less so. This fact, which needs no argument or even illustration, has tended toward the displacement of the home as the center of life and enjoyment. Technological advances and labor-saving devices have added greatly to our conveniences. They have also made possible much greater comfort and luxury. But greater conveniences and comfort necessarily cost more. Homes tend to be affected in at least two ways because of this increased cost, together with the increased need for labor and variety of labor that such cost entails.

For one thing, luxuries of one period become the necessities of the next. We consider as necessities today many things that our grandparents never dreamed of and that our parents thought of as luxuries. This is not entirely because of human greed. Neither does it necessarily stem from the desire "to keep up with the Joneses." Such motivations may be present; but it is also true that when adjustments have been made toward enrichment and comfort in living, the skills, abilities, and sensibilities that made a previous way of living satisfying are lost. The results of these facts on family life are well known. Both men and women may be disposed to delay marriage while both work to procure the means to buy things that their parents got along very well without. Or if marriage is consummated, the bearing of children may be delayed or their number limited while husband and wife earn money to pay for the increased cost of those things which in our generation have become necessities. This situation is particularly true among the great "middle class" of our American society — the class that composes the bulk of our college people and our church people.

A second thing should also be recorded here. Multiplying gadgets for comfort may result in added leisure. And leisure, unless it is used for the enrichment of personality, results in boredom. Professor Tsanoff writes, "The fact is that much of woman's daily work has been taken right out of her hands by organized business." And he adds in the same paragraph that in consequence of this a wife may find her life partly emptied of content, and thus "her dissatisfactions keep pace with her increasing leisure" (p. 204). This is not to decry the multiplication of laborsaving devices for the home. In these days when maid service in the form of built-in conveniences is almost the only help a busy housewife and mother can expect, they are lifesavers! But, these "lifesavers" can also serve as reminders to us that ease and leisure cannot be ends in themselves. Labor-saving devices must not merely free us *from* something that has to be done, they must free us *for* something worth-while. Where they fail to do that, the result is boredom and a sense of uselessness.

In this connection, I should like to say that pity for our grandparents is probably largely wasted — when that pity is expressed on account of the deprivations " down on the farm " or in the " big old house in town " with no conveniences. The very fact that our grandparents did without many of the conveniences which we have come to depend upon so completely meant that they had to find the meaning of life in the daily round of duties. They had no leisure to spend in fruitless boredom. Similarly, it is a waste of breath to urge that people ought to be happy " because they have everything." Having things that release us from drudgery does not bring contentment and happiness. One must never forget that happiness as a conscious experience arises, as all experience must arise, out of the meaning of activity. Only rest or physical renewal arises out of inactivity as such. A positive sense of worth, beyond needed rest, must arise out of a program of activity. Consider the difference between spending three hours at a gay party and spending an equal amount of time at the depot waiting for a delayed bus. The difference of feeling arises because of the activity or inactivity. In the case of the party, one becomes so immersed in a program that time passes unnoticed. In the case of the delayed bus, one's inactivity when rest is not needed results in boredom. Obviously, we cannot make leisure an end to seek. Neither can we imagine that simply having leisure is a possible way to contentment.

Changes such as these are constantly taking place. We cannot and would not stop them. But as such changes affect the family and home we can and should remember that mere added conveniences and more leisure can never reduce the need for a consciously worth-while program of activity. An equal need for both husband and wife to bestir themselves to " keep the wolf from the door " can be a real means toward domestic happiness. So too, the final ability — by mutual effort of husband and wife — to buy a needed appliance can produce for them a greater thrill than the gift of that same appliance could ever be.

The Place of Women in Public Regard

Accompanying the economic and technological changes have been social changes that have tended to affect the place of women in public regard. Consequently, the family has been affected. The changes are subtle and often unrecognized, but they are nevertheless real. In general they have tended to appear disadvantageous to women, often forcing the complaint from women that this is a man's world. The change taking place within the span of a single lifetime could, perhaps, be illustrated in this way: When I was a small lad on the frontier plains of southern Texas, I used to hear a popular doggerel song, some of the lines of which went like this:

> So early, so early, one morning in May,
> I heard an old bachelor imagine and say,
> I don't see what the reason can be
> But none of those girls will marry poor me.

Contrast that sentiment with what I have heard adolescent boys bringing home from school recently:

> She's too fat for me,
> I don't want her,
> You can have her,
> She's too fat for me.

This is senseless doggerel of course, but there are evidences that the glow of knightly adulation of a swain's chosen angel has dimmed somewhat in our day. For one thing, there is a relative scarcity of men available for marriage. This is not great in the over-all situation, but one needs only to read the advertisements directed toward the beautification and allurement of women to realize that business seeks to take advantage of the feeling that a shortage of men does exist. Somewhere I came across an advertisement illustrating what I mean. It presented an attractive woman behind a spider's web — the spider and the fly situation. Underneath the picture was the statement that there is another woman who wants every woman's husband, or something to that effect. This was followed by the injunction to use such-and-such a product calculated to keep the little woman attractive to her husband.

The social fact to which we are calling attention here is this: in our society women are generally expected to wait for proposals of marriage instead of actively seeking such proposals. This fact reduces women's chances of marrying when and whom they please — whether the shortage of men available for marriage is really great enough to be significant or not. No doubt it is an injustice to women to have to wait for men to propose marriage to them. And perhaps the situation requiring women to wait for proposals is changing. At least I am impressed with the fact that in current magazine stories the quest in love has been largely reversed from earlier years. As I remember the stories during my own youth, it was almost invariably the man who pursued the girl; now it is likely to be the girl in pursuit. (Though here I have to admit that I've heard my wife say I only imagine it used to be different.) In any case, it remains true in our society that young women expect men to propose marriage to them; they do not usually expect to propose themselves. Consequently, many women never marry.

Another social factor keeps some women from getting married and often causes women deliberately to refuse marriage when it is offered to them. The stratification of our society decrees that a woman who marries below her social station will suffer more on this account than a man who does the same thing. A woman takes the name and social station of her husband; a man is, relatively speaking, independent of whom he marries. If a socially recognized and brilliant man marries a brainless nobody, she becomes the Mrs. Somebody. But if a socially recognized and talented woman marries a brainless, social nobody, she then becomes the wife of Mr. Nobody. True, she may be able to maintain her social status, but the fact that she married Nobody seems to prove that she isn't anybody much after all, else she would have made a wiser choice.

The consequence of this is that, in general, marriage has a social meaning for women which it does not have for men. In getting married, a young woman has arrived in a sense that is not equally true for her husband. To an important extent the woman has established the pattern for her whole future. The man, on the other hand, has established a relationship of comfort, convenience, and happiness, but he definitely still has his way to make; and, economically at least, making his way seems more difficult because he is married. This seeming difficulty probably accounts in part for the growing evil of wife desertion, which increased by such alarming percentages following World War II.

The Significance of Marriage to Men and Women

Not only is the place of women different from that of men in the eyes of society with regard to marriage, but also in the minds of individuals themselves marriage tends to mean one thing for men and another thing for women. Educators attempting to find the main interest centers of college men and women have found that they are not the same. Among women, men rank first; while among men, business, profession, and lifework rank first. This fact is implied in the paragraphs above, together with the social significance. From a practical standpoint of husbands and wives, this fact has important bearing upon early adjustments among the newly married.

If young wives always understood this difference indicated here, it would probably spare them some of the tears shed when they first discover that husbands choose to remain downtown and have dinner with the boss or an out-of-town customer on a given evening instead of coming directly home on the four-thirty bus — as a husband should if he still loved her as much as he used to! An understanding by the young man of the significance of marriage to his wife could also explain away his bewilderment when he doesn't understand what the wife's tears are all about. The fact is she arrived when she married; he did not.

The Effect of Known Sex Irregularities

A fourth factor must be recorded, and with it we will conclude this chapter. The social consequences of known sex irregularities are greater for women than for men. Men who wish to escape the economic and social responsibilities of marriage can establish illicit relationships with comparative impunity. We have already indicated something of the economic and social responsibilities and their cost. Men may be frightened away from marriage by the cost of a house and its furnishings as well as by the large percentage of the family income that is spent by women, according to published surveys. Men who wish to avoid responsibilities may all too readily engage in sex irregularities.

But women who establish illicit sex relationships are likely to suffer an intolerable social ostracism on account of it. Here, as with other social discriminations mentioned above, is injustice against women, no doubt. But this unjust discrimination by society is a fact just the same in spite of its injustice, and women will do well to remember that it is a fact. Moreover, women as well as men are guilty of making this discrimination; so women themselves are partly at fault.

Some very attractive women turn away from marriage when they consider some of the social factors we have been discussing. This is by their own choice. The disproportion of women to men is by no means so great as to make it impossible for women to marry, the sex drive being what it is. But many women prefer the social and professional achievements possible through their own capabilities to the hazards of social discriminations and misunderstandings such as we have mentioned. And who can blame them?

It is certain that a good and full life is possible to women who choose to remain unmarried. It is equally certain that a woman is foolish who decides to marry just anybody in preference to remaining an old maid. No unmarried woman should feel that her whole world must fall in on her just because she remains single. Long experience and observation convince one that the prospects of some women are less bright because they are married than the prospects of others because they choose to remain single.

Our purpose in this chapter has been to exalt the home by placing it in its proper perspective. If we have succeeded, it will be apparent that the married state is better for mankind than the single state. But it is better only where the person is married to a worthy marriage partner. The fulfillment of sex in the true sense is much more than mere biological fulfillment, important as that is in God's creative plan. True fulfillment includes total growth through all of life's relationships. It includes the flowering and fulfillment of goodness, beauty, truth, and justice as well as security and peace.

CHAPTER

V

Making a Good Marriage

JUST AS THE FAMILY IDEAL persists, so also approval of good marriage is universal. Equally common is the supposition by each individual that he himself is capable of being a partner to a good marriage provided the other partner is equally capable — and provided the other partner is willing to overlook admitted handicaps for which one does not think himself to blame. Still, marriages often fail. And they fail in spite of the sincere promise of marriage partners to take each other " for better or for worse." Something, somewhere, causes the trouble. What is it?

CONDITIONING FACTORS OF A GOOD MARRIAGE

A good marriage is conditioned by many factors. Sometimes these factors are unknown or disregarded by persons entering into marriage. Trouble follows. There is little real excuse for this since many of the conditioning circumstances are easily apparent. Nevertheless, marriages continue to fail because people disregard these factors. Thus we need to mention some of these conditions for further consideration in the context of the study we are making here.

Do Not Expect Perfection in a Partner

A person first of all indicates his capability for making a good marriage when he does not expect to find perfection in the marriage partner he seeks. The romantic eyes of young people in love sometimes see (and thus come to expect) a perfection that does not — cannot in fact — exist. Looking for perfection in a mate may thus cause young people to refuse opportunities for marriage that probably would turn out well. On the other hand, imagining that one has found too great a measure of perfection in the partner one chooses can produce bitterness and disillusionment after marriage. We should remember always that the ideals we have concerning personality are made up out of the experiences we have had of admired characteristics (qualities) in many different individuals. Nobody we have ever met embodies all of our admired qualities. So if one waits for her "Prince Charming" or for his "Fairy Princess," one must remain single. And if courtship and the honeymoon lead one to believe that this ideal has been found, disillusion is sure to follow later on.

This point should be remembered in this connection: since nobody is perfect, no "one and only" individual exists in this world with whom a particular person will be supremely happy and without whom one must necessarily pine away in disappointment and regret. In spite of all the virtues of soap, face cream, toothpaste, and perfume that are often added (especially by women) to the free gifts of nature, certain flaws are bound to remain. Nobody is without some undesirable traits. So, too, no one lives whom one of us could not possibly do without. Rather, on the other hand, romantic songs and fiction notwithstanding, many persons are living with whom any given individual could work out a happily married life if he or she really tried.

Consider Inheritable Factors

Good inheritance is another factor in making a good marriage. I have known young women in college to look up a young man's IQ in the records before accepting a date from him. But the IQ is not very important in itself alone. Those persons who have the highest IQ's may turn out to be very poor marriage prospects, for unfortunately the IQ does not necessarily indicate a person's social or "common" sense. So I have long said that a more important thing to look for in one's marriage partner than IQ is H.S. — H.S. standing for "horse sense."

In any case, a common cause of trouble in marriage is failure to recognize the truth that one marries a family, not simply one individual. This, though unavoidable, seems frequently overlooked. It is commonplace for a boy in love to say that he is marrying the girl, not her mother. Or the girl puts it the other way around and insists that she is marrying the man, not his family. But it isn't really so simple as that. A gracious lady, who provided me with room and board when at sixteen I first went to work in a grocery store in the city, put good advice succinctly when she remarked one morning: "When you are ready to marry, just pick out a woman whom you would like as a mother-in-law. Then, if she has a daughter, marry her!"

There really is something to "this heredity business," and only the foolish disregard it. Physiological and psychological inheritance is a matter to consider. Older persons are constantly aware of startling likenesses between children and their parents when they were the same age. This is so true that young persons can tell very well what their sweethearts will come to look like by looking at the sweetheart's parents. No one should marry John — or Joan — without first knowing what his family is like. The biological and psychological characteristics found in a family are certain to be reproduced. Of course, a given person is a child of his whole family, not merely of his parents; but the factors of inheritance are not changed. The parents contain all the inheritable factors, and what they pass along to a child determines to an important extent what that child can become. Tragedy is the price often exacted where inheritance is disregarded in marriage. Devotion may rise above such tragedy and save the marriage, but even the highest devotion can never be sure of avoiding the tragedy.

Social inheritance is another kind of inheritance of importance. Psychologists remind us that habits determine not only what we do, but also what we want. Consequently, community and family ways of doing things help to determine what an individual wants and what seems natural and right to him in his manner of living. For example, two equally sincere housewives may have very different housewifely routines, which seem right and proper to one but not to the other, because their upbringing was different. The principle here is important in many areas, including marriage. Here, for instance, is one reason for the observed fact that persons with substantially common cultural backgrounds are more likely to be happy together in marriage than persons whose backgrounds are dissimilar. For there are, in fact, family and culturally accepted ways of making love, of furnishing and keeping a room, of preparing a meal. The fact that one is in love with a mate will not keep difficulties from arising where differences exist between them in these respects. Every counselor has listened to distressed wives deplore " his " ways that are enough " to make me scream," and to husbands who declare that " her " ways are enough " to make me take my hat and walk out." To the one complaining, the objectionable ways often seem to be such easily changed patterns of conduct that it seems mere childish stubbornness on the part of the other to continue them. Here, we suggest, is one great barrier to the full success of intercultural and interracial marriages.

The needed caution is this: if you dislike the ways of the parents, have a care lest you marry into them when you choose the son or daughter. Here again devotion may rise above such obstacles and save a marriage, but the price will necessarily include difficult adjustments.

Real Love Based on Friendship

A third factor in the making of a good marriage is the existence of real love between the marriage partners. Or to put it the other way, one cause of trouble in marriage is the failure of the husband and wife to be really in love. Love is, of course, taken for granted in marriage; relatively few people marry who do not imagine themselves in love. But — something else is sometimes mistaken for love. A physical infatuation may be mistaken for love; so also may a desire for security or simple admiration.

Love — real love — is first of all friendship. And it cannot abide the absence of friendship. Infatuation is essentially physical attraction without friendship; and physical attraction, though desirable, is not enough to ensure love. Jeremy Taylor is quoted as having said somewhere that love is friendship set on fire. Physical attraction plus erotic feeling can help to set friendship on fire, but friendship there must be if the blaze is to burn steadily and serve to warm and light a home. A beautiful woman and a man with a physique like a Greek god make a striking couple and provoke excited whispers in a restaurant, but this is by no means enough to guarantee happiness for them as a married couple.

If it is asked, "Isn't friendship just love?" the answer is, "Not necessarily, if what you mean by love is romantic attraction." Friendship means that my friend is interested in what interests me because it interests *me*. Friendship is outgoing, not self-seeking. A man or woman may have a wholly selfish desire to possess a chosen person for self-satisfaction, for self-aggrandizement, or for personal security; but that is different from the friendship feeling that is a necessary bond of a happy marriage. Friendship is genuine mutuality. One confides in his friend — tells him of his hopes and fears, his successes and failures. He confides in his *friend* because he feels that his friend is interested and can be trusted. Nobody confides his inmost hopes and fears to a man immediately upon introduction to him. The old saying, "Don't tell me your troubles, I have enough of my own," applies to strangers; it does not apply to friends. Friends receive their rights, or "just dues," from friends not because friends insist on having their rights but because friends want to safeguard and protect the rights of those they call friends. True, the erotic hunger that demands another for self-satisfaction and for the completion of the creative process is the drive behind friendship, just as it is behind all other social commerce. But, the point is that friendship also includes a readiness to endure pain and self-debasement if that be necessary for the good of a friend. Friendship — friendship as a quality in the relationship between husband and wife — includes the desire to be parents, to have fellowship, to protect and advance the loved one, plus the erotic hunger as such.

In sum, what I am saying amounts to this: what two persons have in *common* guarantees happiness in marriage. The notion is abroad to the effect that opposite personalities attract each other. This is largely a false notion, but it has a grain of truth in it. Imagine a young man interested only in prize fighting and a young woman interested only in embroidery. Suppose they get together on such a basis for an enjoyable evening! The element of truth in the idea is that people always have potential interests, so are always capable of new interests. Moreover, the fact of sex is an all-embracing interest wherein the person of one sex is necessary to the completion of the other. But in spite of this, the fact remains that mutuality, intercommunication between persons, is confined within the limits of what they have in common. Social and personality likenesses, not differences, bind persons together. Just as a musician must communicate his music to another by finding a responsive chord in another, and just as in the absence of such a responsiveness in another he cannot *impose* his music on another, so also a person must communicate — not impose — himself on another. Communion, rapport, happy togetherness — this is shared; it is never merely passed along.

A practical application of this principle of common interests and hopes should be indicated here: nobody should marry merely on the basis of a feeling of obligation to make the marriage partner happy. Young people are frequently in trouble because of a distressing feeling of duty in this respect. They have imagined themselves in love during high school and have exchanged promises or imagined understandings of marriage. Then later on one or the other of the couple finds out that he was not really in love. I suppose everyone who comes in contact with numbers of young people has met cases of this sort. A boy will say, "I am as good as engaged to a girl at home, but now I think I don't love her." Or a girl will say, "I have an understanding with a boy who went to work instead of coming to college, but now I have met a boy who means more to me." What can anyone say to such sincerely troubled young people? Of course they should not have committed themselves in high school. In high school they were probably more in love with " love and romance " than with each other, but suppose they think they are committed?

Of course, the principle we are discussing, that nobody should marry merely on the basis of a feeling of obligation to make somebody else happy, cannot serve as sufficient warrant for breaking an engagement, but it can be a help toward the discovery of what should be done. Persons who think they have found a newer love need to be reminded that perhaps a new flame seems brighter only because it is near at hand and seems warmer because it promises greater self-glorification. There is truth in the old saw, " Absence makes the heart grow fonder — for the one near at hand."

But regardless of how a present dilemma ought to be solved, it remains that people ought not to marry out of a sense of obligation to make another happy. The reason for this is obvious. The only way to make another happy in marriage is to be happy oneself. It is quite impossible to pass such happiness along as one might pass the cake. Happiness in marriage is shared; and in order to share it, one must have it oneself. If one marries another just because of an obligation to make that person happy, he will not fulfill his obligation.

We can hardly overemphasize the necessity for persons to consider the marriage relationship as one of mutuality and complete unity. The fact that some regard the relationship as one of individual rights and duties is responsible for much philandering and so-called sex incompatibility. Coldness and irresponsiveness are more largely attributable to bad humor or to a wrong attitude toward marriage partners than to psychological make-up. That persons differ in romantic interest because of social and psychological factors may be granted, but this is not the real source of nearly so many marital problems as is sometimes thought. The chief offender in the marriage relationship is a wrong attitude toward the mutuality of the relationship. People out of harmony or at cross purposes with each other simply do not attract each other toward the love embrace. Sometimes this also causes disappointment in hopes for children, and further marriage conflicts and frustrations arise in consequence. Doctors frequently advise would-be parents that their trouble may be due to emotional tensions instead of physical problems.

This principle under discussion can, of course, be applied to wider areas than to marriage alone. The poet was right when he said that it is " not what we give, but what we share, for the gift without the giver is bare." Suppose a man is ambitious to be of service and to add to the happiness of mankind. Let him then be first of all happy himself. Happiness is much more easily communicated than conferred. For this reason the happy home is really the end, the culmination, toward which a good society moves. The home is not merely the means for the propagation of the race and the salvation of society. The truth is just the other way around. The home is the end; and, as an end, it becomes a means also. This is so because the good, when seen in the home where the good can be seen at its best, will be seen as desirable and will be sought after. " A city set on a hill cannot be hid." (See Matt. 5:14–16.)

Pride in One's Own Sex

Pride in one's own sex is the last of the factors that we mention here as a condition for making a good marriage. One cause of trouble in marriage — or a cause of trouble in getting married — may be the failure to accept and to take pride in the fact that one's sex is what it is. As this relates to finding a marriage partner and to happiness in marriage, the failure is more likely to be a fault of the female than of the male. Boys are not likely to wish to appear as " just one of us girls "; and few insults to manhood are taken more to heart than the charge of being " effeminate." (We are told by trained counselors that fear of " loss of manhood " and the desire to be convinced that this is not true often underlies romantic escapades on the part of middle-aged men.) In every way men resent being considered less than men. But girls more often appear to seek companionship with boys by adopting boyish ways. No one reason can explain all such attempts. Girls are more likely to resent their sex than boys because of the organization of our society favoring boys. And as we have stated before, society decrees that girls should be chosen by their sex partners instead of choosing their own freely. For these, and other reasons, girls may try to make themselves attractive to boys by seeming capable of boyish interests and ways. But the desire to imitate the opposite sex — where it exists on either side — changes nothing; and instead of attracting, it alienates.

We emphasize here the psychological truth that the whole process of personality development is saturated with awareness of sex differences. Among boys and girls the awareness of one another, as boys or girls, is different from their awareness of others of their own sex. No other fact about a boy or a girl is so attractive to the opposite sex as the fact of sex itself. This is a continuing fact about the relationship of the sexes. In our jury system the supposition is often advanced that women jurors are inclined to sympathize with men and that men jurors are reluctant to "hang a woman." Anybody — man or woman — can easily put the principle to a simple test. Notice how you feel when a woman passes down the aisle or occupies the adjoining seat at a public gathering; then compare this to the way you feel in the case of a man. Sex makes differences everywhere.

To return to the problem with which we began, this means that girls wishing to be attractive to men cannot ignore the fact of sex differences. Normal men certainly are not attracted to weakness in women, that is true. But men are attracted to feminine characteristics; they do not want to marry men. A girl cannot be a sort of good fellow among the boys if she wishes to attract any one of them as something more than a mere companion. Of course, boys may accept girls as companions in fishing and hiking; and, of course, girls can hike and fish with boys without sacrificing their feminine charms. The thing that must not be forgotten is this:

where marriage is contemplated, the social as well as the physical characteristics of the opposite sex count most.

SHALL I GET MARRIED?

Such a discussion as the foregoing would not be complete if further questions were not raised. "Shall I get married?" "If so, how?"

At one time or another marriage counselors are certainly asked whether the person seeking advice should abandon another career for marriage. This is very likely a woman asking, because the careers of men are more independent of marriage. But it may be a man also. As we have suggested earlier, some obligations are universally binding and once assumed cannot be disregarded. Sometimes a man's profession and the hazards or the deprivations of it may appear to constitute such a perfect obligation, which would seem to preclude freely assuming the obligations of marriage. The ministry or mission service might provide examples of such perfect obligations. Likewise one might find such obligation in a deeply conscientious desire to engage in some humanitarian service calling for deprivation or economic sacrifice so great as to make family obligations seem impossible to undertake. What does one do in such circumstances?

Marriage as Obligation and Marital Obligations

Let us turn to the last-mentioned situation first. Of course, nobody can tell another person what he ought to do in a case where his calling makes the fulfillment of family obligations appear impossible. As pointed out elsewhere in these studies, a person's conscience must be his own guide in any present situation. At the same time one can sometimes delay a decision while he weighs factors in the situation that may result in a better judgment regarding it.

From the start one should have in mind that we have, as individuals, no moral obligation to marry just in order to keep the race from dying out. The sex hunger being what it is and the wish (especially among women) to have children being what it is, there is no likelihood that the race will die out because of voluntary refusal to reproduce it. Furthermore, the uncertainties of inheritance are so great as to make it difficult for any one of us to claim that for the benefit of society he must produce a family. We marry for love and for self-fulfillment, not from a sense of duty to mankind. True enough, we think it too bad when a strong and talented man appears unlikely to reproduce himself or when a brilliant and attractive woman with a gift for motherhood appears unlikely ever to become a mother. Still, such considerations do not add up to a moral duty to marry. Marriage is something we choose because we wish, not something we do because we ought.

One should further have in mind that family obligations are perfectly binding moral obligations once they are established. Once one is married he cannot assume other obligations with complete freedom. Marriage forges a mighty, voluntary link in the chain of being. This is the most profound fact about marriage. As we have previously said, in marriage man engages with God in the act of creating persons who become the end and aim of God's entire purpose. Once this link is forged, its obligations and responsibilities become final. This means that a family man must put his family first. He cannot, therefore, maintain obligations to his calling without regard to the sacrifices of family needs unless such sacrifices are willingly made.

A few minutes' reflection should make the meaning of this principle clear. This principle does not mean that a marriage partner may not *willingly* undertake to share the sacrifices and deprivations involved in a partner's calling. It would be withholding a partner's rights to full community of interests to deny full community in sacrifice. Certainly one of the most beautiful things in life is a gifted person who appears ready to pour out his or her gifts — usually hers — with complete self-abandon in obscurity and poverty because that is the life of the partner she has chosen. In such cases the chances are great that the hardships and deprivations suffered by children in the family will be more than compensated for by the beauty and richness of the family relationship. At the same time this principle does mean that a marriage partner cannot *demand* an unreasonable sacrifice on behalf of calling or profession if that sacrifice is not willingly made. For example, if a man were to demand such sacrifice "because he is the boss," or "because he has to make the living," or "because a man's wife ought to do what her husband tells her to do"—a man making such demands would be guilty of unjustifiable domination of his wife. Such domination results in sorrow and loss.

Marriage Versus Other Careers

When we turn to the other question raised at the beginning of this section—that of giving up a career for marriage—the principle is much the same as stated already. This question is obviously a question among girls mainly. The first inquiry a counselor will most likely make of a young woman seeking advice is: "What do you *want* to do? Do you want to be married, or do you want a career?" If she does not know which she wants most, it would seem unlikely that she was much in love. She may be under some kind of social or parental pressure. Or she may wish to make a good marriage. But if she does not want to marry the man more than she wants to do anything else, she is probably not ready for marriage.

This means that a young woman in high school or college should not think of her future solely in terms of marriage and homemaking. In our day the young woman has far too many outside-the-home relationships and responsibilities; she has far too much opportunity to achieve a full and meaningful life—even though marriage may be denied—for her to plan *only* for marriage. And besides, the young woman who fails to prepare herself along some line that might become a career outside the home (if circumstances required it) is not fully prepared for homemaking. A young woman may prefer the career of homemaking and plan toward it, but she should also plan for a different career. If and when the time comes, one can change her career plans for the more preferred one. From time to time young women have brought me this sort of personal problem. I have sometimes told them that when the time comes to surrender a career for marriage they probably will not feel it necessary to ask anybody whether they should do so or not. They will be so anxious to marry the man that the question will not be whether or not to marry, but how soon it can be arranged!

Young women should always plan for a full and active life regardless of marriage. Meaningful living is necessarily active living, for it is activity that gives rise to awareness of meaning. Everyone's face should be set toward a program of living that will be meaningful and satisfying regardless of marital status. Then if marriage is offered, it can take its proper place in the scheme of living; or if in some cases it is not offered, meaningful living can go on without it. Everyone has known unmarried women (and men), young and old, whose lives provide abundant proof that this is possible.

Encouraging a Marriage Proposal

There remains to be considered the case of the girl who thinks she has found "the man" but finds that he does not propose marriage to her. Those whose advice is sometimes sought by young people contemplating marriage will almost certainly be confronted, at some time or another, by a young woman who wishes to discover how dating can be advanced toward marriage. One finds that such women are sometimes contemplating actions regarded as socially irregular at least, if not downright immoral, and they wish advice from an older person.

The obvious first advice to such a young woman is this: you cannot usually advance dating toward marriage by compromising your character, and you can never compromise your moral standard without paying a price. A woman cannot compromise herself without losing something without which it would be scarcely possible to hope for full happiness after marriage. Above all things, happiness in marriage depends on trust of one's partner, and premarital compromise is certainly a poor basis for later trust. Nobody is likely to trust completely the future integrity of a person who falls below the standard in present virtue, honor, or self-respect. By that same token, a man who encourages compromise on the part of his sweetheart but promises to be faithful to her alone once they are married does not deserve to be taken seriously regardless of whatever momentary sincerity he may feel.

But while this has been said by way of caution or determent, something more positive should also be said to the girl who would like to find a suitable marriage partner. What I should like to say here is that one need not be so bashful or noncommittal as not to show any preference for one above another among the eligible men. If a girl really feels a preference for a certain young man, ways will easily suggest themselves by which she can — and should — make it known. Nobody should be so afraid of being considered forward or designing as not to allow the fact that she is attracted toward a person to become apparent to that person himself in direct personal ways.

Religious and Denominational Differences

Finally under this question as to whether or not one should marry, we must bring up the problems arising out of the religious or denominational differences of marriage partners. Such differences raise many of the most serious questions of all. Usually when young people are brought together in general social contacts, they do not fall in love because both are of the same religious faith. They fall in love in spite of sometimes being of quite different faiths. How many problems there are here! And how many homes are seriously disturbed on this account later, because a satisfactory arrangement of religious matters was not worked out *before* marriage!

Troublesome religious disagreement sometimes occurs before marriage because of a tenacious religious loyalty on the part of one or the other proposed partner. Young people should remind themselves in such cases that such a loyalty, in itself, is not an objectionable characteristic in one's marriage partner. I have sometimes talked with young persons who seemed to think that the only reason religious loyalties were disturbing their marriage plans was an unwarranted stubbornness. Granted the possibility that one sweetheart or the other may try beforehand to establish control of the marriage in this way and granted also the possibility of a stubborn loyalty in this respect that is not justified by a practical devotion to the religious group to which a person belongs — it remains true that religious loyalty is in itself a good thing, just as any high loyalty is good.

Young people should remember also that many religious groups consider it practical abandonment of religion itself when their adherents change religious affiliation. Nobody troubled about the religious differences of a partner wants that. Members of Protestant groups, which for this purpose we may call the more liberal groups, often seem to forget this fact. The ones most likely to be guilty of forgetting are members of churches where change from one denomination to another occurs frequently. Sometimes young persons have said to me: "I don't see why the giving up should all be on one side. I am willing to be liberal about the church we shall belong to and raise our children in; why can't he?" But that is by no means always easy. If in one's mind abandoning one's present church affiliation is equal to abandoning religion itself, that is a great deal for the other partner to demand. And certainly it does not help matters to charge one's sweetheart with stubbornness and narrow-mindedness.

Protestant–Roman Catholic marriages are not the only ones subject to difficulty regarding this matter of church loyalty. Doubtless it is among such marriages that the difficulty is most often encountered; but the same trouble often appears elsewhere also, and often is not much easier to deal with. The experience of everyone who has dealt with considerable numbers of young adults includes urgent appeals from married couples troubled over which church to choose for their children, or from couples wishing to be married who are troubled over what they regard as the unreasonable loyalty of one or the other to a particular Protestant denomination.

In general, the trouble that is likely to be encountered in regard to religious differences is great — so great that persons ought not to marry without first coming to agreement about what they will do. Even in cases where the difference is small, for example, the difference between Methodists and Presbyterians, the matter of whose church it is to be *after* marriage needs settlement *before* marriage. One thing sure is that all, or almost all, of those to whom such studies in morals as these are addressed will wish some kind of church affiliation for their children. Not to have an understanding beforehand about such important matters on the ground that " love will take care of everything " is to subject marriage to the possibility of at least two unnecessary hazards: the hazard of serious disunity or else the hazard of drifting toward religious indifference. Both hazards should be, and can be, avoided. A good illustration of what not to do is provided by a couple whom I knew long ago. They attended a Baptist church regularly during their courtship days, that being the home church of the girl. Then, the first Sunday after the marriage, the young husband announced that hereafter they would attend the Presbyterian church, since that denomination was his preference!

Happily, denominational differences are often settled without difficulty on the basis of the preference of one or the other or on the basis of a realistic appraisal of their particular situation. For instance, the location of the home in the community is often a deciding factor. In this country where so many people move from one city or community to another, people who belonged to one denomination in one community may join another in the next place where they live. But — where the matter is a point at issue, the person who regards himself as liberal-minded should remember that whereas he may be ready to meet his or her partner halfway in a solution that represents a change of affiliation for both parties, he may find it necessary to go all the way instead of halfway only. And a considered readiness to do just that may be the price one has to pay for a successful marriage.

CHAPTER

VI

Divorce

THE NUMBER of cases of divorce and its respectability have increased in recent years. These facts are well known. Older persons can remember when it was bad social form to be divorced, but that is by no means true to the same extent now as it once was. The courts used to grant a few divorces in any given year; now they grant hundreds of thousands of them — a half million or more in a given year. Doubtless many things are partly responsible for this changed situation. Social factors have caused some of the change, but since they are factors that we cannot change directly, we need not list them here. At the same time, divorce is a social problem of such staggering proportions that no discussion of marriage and the home can omit consideration of it.

DIVORCE IS EVIL, BUT MAY BE THE LESSER EVIL

In beginning, we should remind ourselves that we would be going to the extreme to say there are *never* circumstances under which divorce ought to be sought — and granted. We *are* correct — and it is easy to say — that young people should exercise greater care before getting married. They should not, of course, get married in circumstances under which it would appear that divorce might likely occur. But the fact is that people sometimes *do* marry under such circumstances in this country where great freedom is allowed to young people in this respect. Having made an unwise choice to marry, young people sometimes believe —

and the courts agree — that divorce is the best way to prevent progressively worse evils from developing.

Again, unforeseeable circumstances sometimes arise that frighten an unstable marriage partner into abandonment of the marriage. The innocent party in such an affair would appear justified in later divorce — and even remarriage if the opportunity was offered. Accidents and diseases are examples of the circumstances we have in mind. I have known wives (and husbands too) who have been victims of abandonment through no fault of their own. Sometimes they were left with small children for whom they could not properly care until they were able to marry again. I have known cases where disease such as hopeless mental illness has been the cause of a broken home. (We are not thinking, of course, of those cases where disease and accidents have been used as *excuses* for abandonment by an unworthy marriage partner.) Besides such cases familiar to everyone, Protestants have always regarded as Scriptural justification for divorce that violation of the marriage vows found in Matt. 19:9.

Some justification does exist for believing that divorce may be the lesser of two evils in some cases. But while this is true, certainly no justification can be found for the idea that divorce is not an evil in itself. Divorce violates the command, "What therefore God has joined together, let no man put asunder" (Matt. 19:6). Divorce hurts everybody involved in it. So in a series of studies such as these, our concern is finding ways in which divorce may be avoided. In this regard, it would be difficult to find anything really new or startling to write, but we can emphasize some obviously sound suggestions, expose some false notions, and indicate some reasons why divorce should be avoided. To these purposes we will devote this chapter.

HOW AND WHY TO AVOID DIVORCE

Avoid Hasty and Trial Marriages

One way to avoid divorce is to avoid hasty marriage. This seems so obvious that everybody will agree to it in principle, and probably few people marry who imagine that they are getting married hastily. Still, sex attraction is strong. And the need for romantic fulfillment of love is so great at times as to cause ill-considered marriages to take place. This being so, it would seem that the very least service that adult advisers of young people could be expected to render is to make counsel against hasty marriage so much a part of youth training that young people cannot easily avoid it. In premarital counseling we find a clear application of the general principle that guidance comes too late where none is provided until such time as an important occasion arises requiring such guidance. All youth need to be cautioned against hasty marriage — whether or not they are currently in love. Yet in far too many cases such guidance is postponed until it is actually sought after by young people. And of course, most young people in love do not feel that they personally need such advice; consequently they do not seek it.

Here we would point out that a vicious but subtly attractive idea is abroad that often encourages hasty marriage. It is to the effect that if people marry and find out afterward that they do not like the marriage, they can be divorced and try again. This seems to imply that marriage is at first a trial affair that can be ended without too much difficulty. Marriage provides a woman with the magic title "Mrs.," and a man with a sense of conquest. Marriage offers to both the man and the woman companionship, various conveniences, and the opportunity for unrestrained sexual indulgence — so the urge to get married is strong. For the same reasons, the hurt and bitterness of possible divorce sometime in the indefinite future may not appear to be a very strong reason against going ahead with marriage now, "Right now, while we wish it so much." How could so natural a course be dangerous or wrong? Yet experience readily provides enough instances where such a "natural" course of action has led to later divorce. The fallacy of this attractive idea is subtle, but it is real.

In this connection it would be well to give further consideration to the hurt and bitterness of divorce. To a young couple contemplating a hasty marriage, the possibility of hurt may not seem strong. Therefore, we say emphatically: divorce hurts, terribly! As a matter of course, divorce requires exposure in court of the details of conduct put forward as justification for the divorce action. This involves charge, countercharge, and recrimination. Such things are not pretty; they are ugly and embarrassing.

But another hurt is greater than public embarrassment, although it is less obvious. That hurt results from the consciousness of one's failure in life's most important social relationship. If one is so inconsequential a person as to be unable to keep the confidence and loyalty of the one to whom he or she has given everything, how is it possible to hope for success in social relationships anywhere? The easy approach to divorce in popular fiction is far from being true to life in fact. Fiction is likely to exploit the idea that dissatisfied married people can approach divorce " as mature and reasonable people. " But in life it simply does not usually work that way. One or the other — usually it is both — is bound to approach the prospect of divorce with immaturity, if by immaturity is meant great emotional disturbance. And such disturbance, since it exists in one partner, is sure to be communicated to the other. If the question is asked, " Cannot two people separate in full mutual respect one for the other? " the answer, I think, must be " No." There can be no regarding marriage as if one could easily get out of it after it has been consummated.

Do not marry hastily. Be sure you are right before you go ahead. A married person is very much married!

Not only because of the hurt of divorce, but also for a further reason, hasty or ill-considered marriages should be avoided. Likely there will be children whose rights are jeopardized whenever divorce is sought by their parents. Everybody knows that children are the greatest and most pathetic victims of broken homes. However, not all young people consider prospective children a reason for delay and caution before marriage. Indeed, in the case of young men, the urgency of sex itself plus other obvious advantages of marriage, not the prospect of children, is usually foremost in mind. In so far as children are concerned, most young men probably do not love their children before they are born. They feel fully confident of their ability to become fathers at any convenient time during marriage. Even when children are in prospect, they are probably more concerned about the wife and her approaching ordeal than they are about the child. They may want children in general but still be unable to imagine the particular child still unborn as necessary to fulfillment of that desire. Thus it is that young men contemplating marriage are not driven by a desire to establish a home. Sex causes young men to press for marriage at the earliest possible moment; young men want to possess their women.

Similarly, young women who are disposed to rush headlong into marriage are driven by something else besides real eagerness to establish a home and to have children. They too may be driven by sex. Or they may have an urgent desire to escape from a present home situation; or, being more in love with "love and romance" than with the duties and responsibilities of marriage and parenthood, they may be driven by romantic dreams to want marriage "right now."

But even if only lightly considered *before* marriage, likely there will be children whose rights should be considered when a hasty marriage is contemplated. *After* marriage, women will usually want children and feel dissatisfied and progressively frustrated if none are born. Sometime after marriage, husbands also (in many cases) may feel that their wives are failing them if an heir is not presented to them, particularly so after the husband has attained some economic or professional success. Moreover, the fact that a man does not become a father may seem to be a reflection on his manhood — a situation a man usually cannot imagine is justified by the facts. And if this is not true in a particular case of a man, his wife, likely as not, will imagine it is and will feel inadequate on that account. So there will likely be children, or some disturbance to the marriage if there are none. All these probabilities should be taken into consideration before marriage. The prospective rights of children should be considered. So should the added tragedy that children's inevitable suffering gives to divorce. Thus the idea of being willing to try anything once is utter folly when applied to marriage. Far too much is at stake to be willing to approach marriage with "easy" divorce in the back of one's mind.

Beyond these considerations of the hurtful consequences of divorce, there are important social consequences too. Professor Tsanoff calls attention to the fact that, historically, marriage was to a large extent a clan or family affair. In the ancient Japanese civilization, for example:

> Too intimate devotion of husband and wife to each other was frowned upon as unseemly. It was even held as sufficient ground for divorce, which was arranged by the clan elders. Fathers- and mothers-in-law would decide that the excessive love of the pair for each other affected their right loyalty to the larger interests of their allied families (p. 192).

Tsanoff does not, of course, suggest the propriety of a return to such an excessive family view which neglects "the intensely personal and intimate character of the family bond." But the example does "illustrate by sharp contrast the unsocial individualism that is rampant in the domestic morals of our modern age." (P. 192.) The modern marriage sorely needs the addition of a strong consciousness of the social consequences of the marriage relationship. "Modern youth," says Tsanoff, "have shaken loose from the tyranny of the old rigid order, but in their loose thought and practice many of them seem bent toward anarchy." (P. 193.) The family is the basic unit of society; it is the end for which society exists, as we have insisted. But families must live in society if personalities are to come to fulfillment as persons, since persons are known and judged as persons in society. Indeed, society provides persons the standards by which they must judge themselves as persons.

When all these facts are considered, certainly the social relationships and social consequences of a marriage contract between two persons cannot be taken lightly. It is foolish to claim that a given marriage is the sole concern of the contracting parties. This should be fully understood by young people contemplating marriage on the basis that divorce is an easy way out if necessary.

Divorce Should Be Considered as Final

A second suggestion for avoiding divorce is this: realize that divorce, when it comes, is final; it is not just part of the process of getting married to someone else. Divorce writes finis; it is not a proper part of a new adventure in marriage. Even in cases (such as we have referred to) where divorce may be the lesser of two evils and where remarriage may follow sometime later, remarriage should never be a reason for seeking divorce. As a general rule if the reasons for divorce are not compelling enough to have brought it about, then having become attracted to another possible marriage partner is not sufficient reason for seeking divorce. What I mean here is that before divorce is sought, the reasons for seeking it should be final in themselves without the added weight of a desire to marry again.

This may sound like a strong statement, especially in the light of newspaper reports of events surrounding some divorce proceedings. The reason for such a strong statement as this is in the marriage vows themselves and the obligations there assumed. The vows include taking each other for better and worse, richer and poorer, in health and sickness, till death. Such vows are quite inclusive of circumstances and time. They are also exchanged exclusively between two, and only two, people. Nobody taking the marriage vows would go through with the ceremony if one partner said, "I promise to love and cherish you until I see where I think I can do better." And nobody would complete the marriage if his or her partner said, "I promise to be fairly faithful; or faithful three fourths, or even nine tenths, of the time." The promises are to keep oneself for the other *alone* and *always!* Nobody who has taken such vows took them with reservations, nor has one a right to add reservations afterward. I repeat, I do not mean to say a divorced person should never under any circumstances get married again. But what I do insist upon is that divorce ought not to be sought unless the reasons for it are compelling; and a present wish to remarry could tend strongly to bias one's judgment as to whether the reasons are compelling.

In lectures to college seniors during many years I have gone even farther. I have said that a married man or woman who still regards himself or herself as eligible for the sex love of another person is in this respect a fool! Unwittingly, perhaps, he or she is threatening to bring about a whole chain of evil consequences which no wise person would dare risk.

We can add other reasons why divorce should be considered as final, without thought of remarriage. For one thing, one's second choice of a marriage partner cannot be guaranteed beforehand as wiser than one's first choice. If one's first choice was wrong, the odds are against the second choice being any better. What I mean can be illustrated in a more positive way. Suppose a typical married man, completely undisturbed by anger, jealousy, frustration, and the like, were to take his place at the entrance to a department store or supermarket to watch the women come and go. Suppose that in doing this he was trying to see how many of the women, on first impression, appeared as a better marriage prospect than his present partner. He would probably return home feeling he had made a very good choice in his *present* wife!

Again, many persons seeking divorce contend that they are improperly matched. They seem to think that marriage with some other partner might have been different. Some, no doubt, have in mind that they will later remarry. The actual claims in the divorce may read "incompatibility of temperament," "mental cruelty," and "coldness." Usually what such claims amount to are nothing more than confessions of a bad temper. That there are wide variations of personal characteristics among persons is readily granted, but the differences that interfere with a satisfactory marriage relationship are mostly temperamental, not physiological. True, persons of the same sex are not as alike as "two peas in a pod," but they are alike in basic nature. If this were not so, a science of biology, a science of psychology, and a practical science of medicine would not be possible. Basic structures, hungers, reaction patterns are common to us all. The chief differences are in *qualities of spirit* wherein we ourselves are responsible. In these qualities growth, change, and development are possible. So when most poorly adjusted marriage partners seek a change of partners for what they contend are physical reasons, what they need more is a change of heart.

This point — the thought that life might be better with a different partner than the present one — needs emphasis because this is a reason most often given why married people become involved in the " marriage triangle " which is so common to current fiction writing and to life itself. One wonders sometimes what fiction writers would do for plots if the triangle were not so easily available and so obviously ready-made. There can be no doubt that triangle situations do exist; and the ready-at-hand reason for them is that of which we have been writing: married people feel frustrated in love, or they feel cheated out of marriage thrills such as they may have experienced during the honeymoon, and they imagine that someone else could provide such love and thrills to them permanently. Feeling cheated, they justify themselves in beginning what is at first — but seldom remains — a mild philandering. In such cases the original frustration was probably due largely to a feeling of starved ego, and this same feeling is likely to cause an attempt to achieve satisfaction by way of the sex conquest of another person.

Wrong thinking in respect to the triangle situation is encouraged by a popular false notion — a notion that often is also a factor in hasty or ill-considered marriage in the first place. I refer to the false notion that falling in love is a sudden and a well-nigh overwhelming experience. Now love at first sight may not be impossible, but certainly that is not the way most people have come to be in love. The idea that one suddenly saw " the one and only " across the room at a party and instantly was hopelessly in love — this may make a good song or story (although even here one might wonder if, and why, it would be less likely to happen across the bus station than at a party). But falling in love is not likely to be the instantaneous chemical reaction, triggered by a mutual glance, that makes romantic fiction sound romantic. In actual fact, love usually follows a passing attraction that has been cultivated. In spite of protestations, this is most likely how the triangle develops. A wife or husband whose ego is flattered by attention of the opposite sex meets an acquaintance — or makes an acquaintance — and shares a pleasant hour. Then the acquaintance is cultivated until the triangle situation develops.

If argument were needed to prove the above observation, it could be found in the manner young people usually employ in selecting their marriage partners in the first place. Many occasions bring young people together; there follows a succession of "dates." In most cases the first date is not a completely overwhelming experience. It is simply a pleasant and stimulating evening that could have been forgotten but was in fact repeated. It was repeated because it was pleasant, not because the boy and girl had fallen hopelessly in love with each other. It is the repeated dating and the good times young people have in each other's company that results at last in their being in love. Of course they may quite suddenly realize they are in love, but they did not fall in love suddenly. Likewise, marriage partners are not as a rule suddenly trapped in a love triangle. They enter the triangle because somehow they feel themselves justified in doing so; they feel eligible for the sex love of another person.

Why doesn't a marriage partner consciously try instead to remain attractive to the one whom it once seemed all-important to attract? If that were done, casual or friendly social relationships would not be allowed to progress beyond their first professed intent.

A Conscious Effort to Be Attractive

Actually, our question has suggested a third way of avoiding divorce. One of the most beautiful ties that bind a marriage relationship into a completely harmonious union is the conscious effort on the part of both parties to be attractive in dress and manner to each other. Certainly it is a good thing for a woman to hope she may be attractive to people generally in her dress and manner both out of respect for herself as a person and as a compliment to her husband, so nobody can object when she tries to look her best on the street and elsewhere. But of no less importance is her attractive appearance to her husband when he is at home in the evening and before he leaves for the office in the morning. Familiarity is not enough! Certainly it is a good thing, also, for a man to appear at his best downtown out of respect to himself as a person, as a compliment to those he meets, as a business and professional asset, and as a compliment to his wife and family. But of no less importance is his appearing shaved, bathed, and properly groomed at home. How marriages are able to survive in spite of the appearance of some wives during the morning when nobody is supposed to be looking, or how a woman's love can continue in spite of the dress and manner of the day-at-home of some men — these are marvels! If hard-pressed wives insist there is not time to be neat and attractive or if careless husbands insist that the slovenly way is more comfortable, the answer is that slovenliness is not really necessary, as is proved by countless busy wives and husbands who do not fall into slovenly habits. Furthermore, the answer is that a conscious and persistent effort to be personally attractive to each other pays big dividends in the direction of establishing the kind of home for which we all wish and hope.

Find Marital Happiness in Mutual Activity

Our last suggestion of a way to avoid divorce also exposes a false notion and offers a positive corrective. Married people go astray in their thinking when they imagine marriage is the accomplished state of affairs out of which happiness should automatically arise. Happiness *nowhere* arises merely out of a state of affairs! This we have said before in another connection, but it bears repeating. Happiness as a conscious experience arises as a by-product of activity of some sort; rest and physical renewal are the only desirable results that can come from the cessation of activity. Forgetting or being ignorant of this, married people by their actions often seem to be saying, "I am now married to the man or woman of my choice in all the world; therefore now, let happiness arise." When it does not — as of course it cannot — the honeymoon is gone down and the hoped-for spontaneous romance and excitement of marriage are gone. Marriage then becomes routine, taken for granted much as the daily shopping or the job is taken for granted, and the glamour fades.

A well-known psychological principle comes into play here. Two distinguishable processes are involved in a program of activity. One is the focusing of attention on an object in order to perform an activity; the other is the effect on us which performance of the activity produces. If attention is focused on effect to the extent that interference with the performance occurs, no effect will be forthcoming because performance causes the effect. The feelings we have are by-products of actions; they accompany the effects following from performance of activity. So, too, happiness is a by-product of actions. Happiness sought as happiness cannot be found; as something standing by itself alone it exists nowhere. Focusing attention on happiness interferes with activity that might otherwise produce an effect accompanied by the feeling of happiness. This is true of happiness of any kind; and happiness in love and marriage is like happiness everywhere else in this respect.

It follows that to avoid divorce and to find marital happiness a couple should continue to engage in activities of mutual interest. Observation of young people newly in love ought to be a sufficient reminder that love is such a program of living, not a mere state of affairs. I have often challenged young people to try imagining John and Mary — any John and Mary — who are very much in love. Picture each one alone in his own room rejoicing in the fact of being in love, and each content to sit alone and rejoice. Things are never that way! People in love are constantly doing something, usually together, in consequence of their mutual love. So obviously, if married people quit saying and doing the things that caused them to fall in love with each other and still expect married happiness to be sustained by the mere fact of physical union plus mutual sharing of household duties and responsibilities, they are sure to be disappointed. It was not such a prospect as that which first produced love. Instead, it was the whole person engaging in activities that fell in love, and the whole person is necessary to love's continuance.

But can the trembling excitement of young love and the first weeks of marriage go on forever? The answer is "No." Who would wish that? But the fact that one is in love bears endless repeating. Little time and effort are needed to say, "I love you." And the acts of courtesy, kindness, and mutual consideration that characterize sweethearts need only continued practice to become fixed patterns of conduct. Of course, nobody feels "on top of the world" always; certainly differences and disagreements between married couples will occur; no doubt times of sorrow and tragedy will come when self-pity will cause loss of proper perspective. But — it is never impossible to recall and put into practice the simple principle that the acts, words, and attitudes which brought love about at first will, if continued, preserve it to the end of life. A fully happy marriage never simply happens; it is always achieved.

Some years ago a Y.W.C.A. secretary visited our campus and made an address at chapel entitled "Campus Ghosts." One point I always remembered. It was to the effect that one sort of campus ghost acquires ghostliness by leading people to imagine they can draw life out of situations, whereas it is only possible to put life into situations. Perhaps she should have used the word "demons" instead of "ghosts," but her emphasis was certainly properly placed when she insisted that it is in the doing that we have life. The meaning of life arises as an accompaniment of what is done. For this reason I have often said that people without purpose and program are dead and do not know it. Certainly this applies to happiness in marriage. Happiness is not abstracted from the married state but is built into it by the activity of the man and woman concerned.

Divorce may not always be avoided, as we have said. But the results when divorce is avoided — avoided by conscious effort to make a marriage succeed — the results are worth all the cost. Results add up to *home!* And home is the word for the highest ideal of human welfare that minds have yet conceived or seem likely to conceive in the future. Homes, in the fullest meaning the word has for developing human persons as immortal personalities — homes are the aim of creation; and God, the Ultimate Reality, is Father.

CHAPTER VII

Citizenship

Home is man's first and greatest means to personal fulfillment, his greatest means of security, and consequently (as we have pointed out) requires his first duty before all other obligations. But we have also indicated that man must find his fulfillment in society. Next to the home, man's broader social relationships of life consist of his church, community, and state (state in the inclusive sense of all levels of civil government). In all these relationships the broader meaning of selfhood finds fulfillment.

THE INCLUSIVE NATURE OF CITIZENSHIP

What has been called the divine spark in man includes a hunger for social relationships and social approval. This part of man is what we speak of when we say that man is a child of God; it is the characteristic exhibited in man which a psychiatrist would probably refer to as "the eternal *erōs*." The importance of this hunger for inclusive social relationships is seen in the fact that it is a means to the end by which a man can know himself as a person. We cannot think of ourselves in the abstract. Just as all knowledge comes by comparison and contrast, so we know ourselves as we sustain certain relationships with other persons (or God) wherein we compare ourselves with them. We come to know ourselves as we see ourselves, as doing things either better or worse than others doing the same things.

Ethical writers and psychologists have long insisted upon the importance of society to the individual's self-awareness and his self-fulfillment. The ideals that we try to fulfill, and to which we compare our achievement, are made up of the admired characteristics seen in others. Even our concept of God — in so far as we can have a concept of him — is arrived at by thinking of God as actively engaging in the exercise of good. The conception of good as a character trait could not exist apart from that good which arises out of good acts. If God is thought of as a person, he must be thought of as actively engaging in good. Thus, Thomas Aquinas concluded that God is pure act.

The principle implied indicates the importance of social relationships to a person's awareness of ideals; and in turn, to a person's sense of self-fulfillment as ideals are progressively embodied in ways of acting in community with other persons. When a person sees in other persons ways of acting that are worthy of admiration, such ways tend to become his ideals. And as he is able, progressively, to embody those ways himself, he moves toward conscious self-realization. In this connection, it is a striking fact that as a farmer, for example, compares himself with other farmers for a sense of self-fulfillment, he does not feel inferior because he is not like a physician, a minister, or a groceryman. These others are not the ideals that he is attempting to fulfill. But at the same time that this is so, the farmer does have ideas about what a physician, a minister, or a groceryman ought to be, even though he feels no need to embody those professional characteristics in himself. Still, the farmer's ideals for others are significant. All of a man's social relationships become a part of his self-awareness and, hence, a means to his self-realization.

It is in this context that we shall discuss society as basic to the needs of men. And as we are thinking of citizenship in this chapter, we are thinking of the individual's relationship not only to civil government but also to the other groupings of society to which he belongs outside the home.

SOCIETY — A BASIC NEED

The Church — A Religious Society

The church, next to the home, provides the means for the most meaningful social relationships available to man. When we become religious, the most important new thing in our experience of self-fulfillment is that we become members of a community — a society — capable of providing us with a set of relationships more inclusive than those of the home.

Here we need to guard against a false notion. There is a false notion that Christian living must be preceded by a God-sent, transforming experience and that in the light of that experience a person undertakes the duties he must perform in order to get to heaven. The Christian faith does not require us to believe that God will " pour out his blessing upon us " in a special sort of experience, as one might pour water on a wilting plant and cause it to revive and grow. Revival preachers of the past were sometimes understood to think this was so. They insisted that religion was, as they put it, " a sensible experience." Or they said, " When a man gets religion, he knows it." A certain emotional experience was necessary to get religion.

Now it is true that important life decisions are characterized by changed emotional states, but nobody needs to wait for a " certain feeling " before he declares his purpose to live the Christian life and before he joins the Christian community. Feeling, of course, motivates further action, and that action will sustain or enhance the feeling of God's presence. But even so, it is action that causes the feeling in the first place. Thus, the way of living — the action — a Christian undertakes must be thought of as the source of satisfying religious experience.

The practical meaning of what I am saying is this: What Christians do in their capacities as churchmen makes up the program of living out of which arises the conscious ability to think well of themselves. When one accepts Christ, he becomes a part of a fellowship; he does not simply accept a set of obligations that will get him to heaven. He acquires a group of friends among whom each is for all and all are for each. When he joins a church, he becomes a member of a face-to-face group in which relationships are, in many respects, like the intimate — brother, sister, kindred — relationships of family. He also becomes a citizen of a world-embracing fellowship — a society — in which his particular church enables him to express ideals and hopes on a world scale. Thus the church provides the individual with abundant means for self-fulfillment, and one finds the " abundant life " in consequence. This abundant life Christians call " freedom in Christ." It is both freedom and duty. Obviously it is freedom in the sense that it is the kind of living that the Christian desires as the way to conscious self-fulfillment. It is duty in the sense that by means of such living God saves mankind, and one who would desire God's purposes fulfilled is obligated to live in this way.

The church provides us with wider relationships of the kind we experience in the home. In the church, even as in the home, duties are the same set of activities as those we call privileges. That which we feel obligated to do is that which we feel privileged to do in order to experience self-fulfillment. In the church we find a set of relationships that become increasingly meaningful as practice turns them into habits; and habits, as the psychologists remind us, determine not only what we do but also what we want.

We can express in another way the need and value of the church relationship. To be completely homeless is the worst fate that could befall a person. But next to that is a fate nearly as sad: living outside the fellowship of the church. The extent of personal loss that may result from remaining outside is, doubtless, not often fully realized by those who suffer the consequences. Their lives have remained empty in this regard, so they are unaware of what is missed. Nevertheless, the value of church relationships is great, and the values increase with the passing years because they relate that which is passing to that which is considered eternal. This ability of relating the present, passing scene to the eternal is one important secret of an abiding sense of well-being for an individual.

So the need for, and the value of, the church is important in many ways for the individual's fullest living.

The Community and Nation — A Civil Society

Less intimate and meaningful than one's church is another set of relationships the individual sustains. These are the relationships in the community — both the immediate and the wider community — in which the Christian lives. The community, of course, is where one lives. It also includes the place where one works and the professional fellowship of which he is a part. The wider community includes the state. In such social groups as these we exercise what is usually called our citizenship (although in this chapter we have used this term more broadly).

Everybody sustains relationships of this sort in some way, and their importance to our sense of self-fulfillment is indicated by the loss men feel when they are deprived of what they understand to be their " rights " in such relationships. Basic philosophy regarding these relationships differs greatly in many respects; whole books are written on the subject. However, the importance of this area of our social functioning is not minimized. For example, at one extreme is the social philosophy of the German Georg W. F. Hegel (1770–1831), who considered such social relationships so all-embracing that he regarded the state as the highest human obligation and opportunity. Such extreme emphasis on the state caused Sören Kierkegaard (1813–1855) and others to revolt against Hegel's system and to propose other interpretations. In the case of the Danish Kierkegaard and others, they proposed the God of revelation as the ultimate fact determining social organization and responsibility. In the case of the existentialists, the ultimate nature of the individual is the determining factor.

But whatever basic philosophy of the state men profess, they do live in communities and they exercise *there* what we call citizenship. And everywhere the relationships of citizens are matters of deep concern, because such relationships have so much to do with the attainment of what people feel they would like to be and to have by way of conscious self-fulfillment. These relationships are deeply involved in two ideals most cherished by persons: freedom and opportunity. For these reasons at least, the state becomes a necessity to the individual; and as such a necessity, it is seen as good. If seen as good, then all citizens are under moral obligation to the state, for morally man is obligated to seek the good.

The conclusion just stated is not everywhere accepted, and indeed it cannot be accepted without some qualifications. For one thing, we are aware that early philosophers of democracy (and of other forms of limited and responsible government) held the state to be a necessary evil. For example, the Englishman Thomas Hobbes (1588–1670) thought all men were, by nature, entitled to all things. But this is impossible, since men would become involved in mutual destruction as they all tried to get the same things. To avoid destruction, Hobbes contended, a compromise must be made for mutual protection; and thus some kind of government is established to which people give a limited loyalty. This sort of thinking has entered deeply into American ideas. We still speak of government by compromise and we still often find ourselves saying, "The best government is the least government"—thus placing government in the category of a necessary evil.

For another qualification, it is true that loyalty to government may conflict with personal moral ideals and with conscientiously held religious convictions. To illustrate, the state may require military service where the private conscience requires refusal to fight. Or, the diplomatic facts of a situation among nations may require duplicity, where private conscience regards all lying as evil. In all such conflicts between the state and the private consciences of its citizens, the state holds a great advantage by being able to compel obedience by force. Thus what we call in this country "the rights of citizens" are likely to be invaded; and we are constantly reminded that "eternal vigilance is the price of freedom." In practice, however, criminals often seek to escape justice by employing the safeguards that have been written into our form of government against the invasion of private rights — as in some use of the Fifth Amendment.

So it is that a constant struggle goes on to "purify" government. What is sought when we think of purifying government is likely this: we think of bringing politics (which is "the science of the possible") more into line with our ideal morally. If citizens could accomplish this aim, then government would seem to be a good thing instead of a necessary evil. But until that aim is possible, many conscientious people feel that they are entitled to withhold their loyalty and obedience to the state on the grounds of conscience; that is, they consider the state an evil as it presently exists.

To a further clarification of the moral obligation of the citizen to the state (consistent with our conclusion a few paragraphs above) we shall now turn.

Private Conscience and Civil Requirements

Considerable confusion starts at this point, when a man's conscience conflicts with that which the civil government requires of him. The basic difficulty is due to two things: expecting the impossible of government and conditioning one's *complete* obedience on the government's achieving what we expect. On first glance it would seem that the government is wrong if it requires of the individual that which violates his conscience. Historically, democratic forms of government are based on the assumed inalienable worth of the individual. This seems in keeping with moral and religious convictions that the individual person is the ultimate value — the individual soul is "the man for whom Christ died."

But a fundamental difference must be recognized here. Political democracy and moral democracy are not the same. Political democracy can recognize the difference, but it can never overcome it completely. A political democracy is "government of the people, by the people, and for the people." A moral democracy would be achieved only if full justice and the rights of *every* individual were brought to pass. A government can no more achieve this ideal than the individual can ever fully achieve his own moral ideal. This is true for many reasons, and we have not space to argue the point fully. Suffice it to say that one important reason is that the rights which are due to persons in a society are constantly changing with the changing environment and circumstances. "New occasions teach new duties. . . . They must upward still, and onward, who would keep abreast of Truth." (James Russell Lowell, "The Present Crisis.") This point will become clearer as we continue the further sections of this chapter.

Approaching the problem in this way one can see the kind of considerations that lead us to the conclusion that no form of government can be perfect from the viewpoint of an ideal moral standard. But while the state cannot possibly be an unqualified good, this does not mean that it is necessarily evil either — the least government being best. It does indicate that representative government is the form most favorable to the realization of the highest moral and religious ideals. Representative government, we say, rests on "the consent of the governed." This idea can be an adequate foundation on which to build a public order from a moral viewpoint but only on the condition that it rests on a belief that a fundamental principle of truth and justice exists which is a part of the nature of things and that the mind can apprehend and act upon that principle. If truth and justice are really a part of the nature of things and if individuals are seeking to embody that reality in living, then a government representing such individuals has a solid basis. But if truth and justice are *not* real, the meaning of the words varying with each individual, then a government representing a group of individuals has a basis that shifts from day to day as the representatives vary their individual and collective opinion of truth and justice.

Thus, democratic government as we know it rests finally on an ideal, or a religious, conviction about the nature of reality. So also, the truth and justice sought by the individual conscience is not unlike that sought by what the government requires of its citizens. Seeming conflicts are the result of changing circumstances and of the failure of individuals—singly and in society—to achieve the ideal. But in spite of this, a civil society assists the individual in his striving for self-fulfillment, as we have said.

THE STATE AND INDIVIDUAL JUSTICE

A further clarification of what we have been saying should result from a further consideration of what we mean by civil justice and law. Throughout these studies our approach has been from the moral and religious point of view—and will continue to be. But with regard to civil matters, this is not the only approach. So our position must be made clear.

Civil Justice and the Popular Will

Civil justice is more than mere popular will. People who believe in government by decree will not, of course, agree. But even many who believe in government by law instead of by decree may not agree. They may take refuge in a philosophy that holds that law is law *only* because it represents what people want; and that law remains law only so long as it represents what people want. The likeness of law to such abstract considerations as good or justice—this, they say, is beside the point or a downright false notion.

But this idea that justice is popular will and nothing more is inadequate as a basis for civil law for the same reason that it is inadequate as a basis for government in the first place (as indicated in the preceding section). Civil laws (as with social and moral) that control us and that are subject to change must be regarded as efforts—never completely successful—in the direction of bringing about a greater good, a good that is real and not subject to the whims of individual men. So civil justice is more than mere popular will. How else could democratic support of law and custom be obtained?

I know the answer given to this sort of reasoning by the late philosopher and educator, John Dewey (1859–1952). He would say that the individual is created by society and has no residue of individuality beyond that conferred on him by biological nature. That means the individual has no real hunger for individual self-fulfillment that goes beyond the limits prescribed by biological nature and by society. Dewey says:

> The idea of a natural individual in his isolation possessed of full-fledged wants, of energies to be expended according to his own volition, and of a ready-made faculty of foresight and prudent calculation is as much a fiction in psychology as the doctrine of the individual in possession of antecedent political rights is one in politics. (John Dewey, *The Public and Its Problems: An Essay in Political Inquiry,* p. 102; Gateway Books, 1946.)

I know also the views of the late Supreme Court Justice Oliver Wendell Holmes (1841–1935). On one occasion he expressed doubt that the word "justice" should remain in mind as an ideal toward which law courts seek to move in their interpretation of law. He said:

> I often doubt whether it would not be a gain if every word of moral significance could be banished from the law altogether, and other words adopted which should convey legal ideas uncolored by anything outside the law. . . . There is a concealed, half-conscious battle on the question of legislative policy, and if anyone thinks that can be settled deductively, or once for all, I only can say that I think he is theoretically wrong. (Quoted by Herbert W. Schneider in *A History of American Philosophy,* pp. 562–563; Columbia University Press, 1946.)

The courts then, according to Justice Holmes, instead of trying to bring about something called justice, should be content to bring to pass whatever is required by law. This will be a *changing* justice "according to law," since law expresses the will of those who make the law valid by their approval.

This is a pragmatic view of what the individual is and what, in consequence, justice is. But this cannot satisfy a religious man — at least not a Christian. (John Dewey, it will be remembered, was concerned about the values of religion but as a naturalist in his philosophy was not Christian.) This view cannot satisfy a physical scientist who believes in the reality of law in the nature of things — at least in statistical law. Nor can this view satisfy a psychologist who believes that mind exists as part, an ingredient, of the real. So we are by no means alone in rejecting the views of such eminent men as Dewey and Holmes.

In fact, there has been a violent reaction to these views in religious circles. The result has been a more dogmatic approach to revelation as the source of authority in morals. This has been among Christians who take either a pragmatic or an existentialist view of psychological and other scientific truth. At the same time a reaction has been going on in certain legal circles against such a pragmatic view of justice as that represented by Justice Holmes. The limits of space and of purpose do not permit a discussion of these here.

The practical purpose intended here also excludes elaboration of the reasons (aside from authoritarian ones) for believing that a democratic social order must rest finally on the conception of law as law, and the reasons for believing that justice is a demand which individuals make upon society because they are individual men, not because they are parts of a social whole. But the sum of it all, as I see it, is this: the culture we know as democratic society could not be expected long to outlast abandonment of a view of truth and justice which is, in its main outlines, religious. Such a view is the main intellectual support of a democratic social order. Such an order must assume that moral and legal requirements will be observed because they represent efforts to move toward truth and justice as parts of the nature of things.

Democratic institutions depend on the will of the people for their stability. People must *want* to meet the requirements of society, otherwise such requirements become a means to individual frustration instead of individual fulfillment. This is true because no matter how deeply the roots of individual consciousness may be imbedded in the soil of society, it remains a fact (Dewey notwithstanding) that the individual knows himself as a person, a single self. He is never independent of society, but likewise he is never fully accounted for by society.

Civil Law and Individual Freedom

What we have said thus far about justice and law leads us to a further point. In democracy, civil law is not a set of restraints interfering with individual freedom. Indeed, probably the greatest danger to democracy which we face is the widespread feeling that moral and civil law are restraints imposed on personal freedom. Instead of restraints to freedom, laws are guideposts toward the desired freedom. Too many people regard the law as the policeman's law. They think it binding on the individual only when it is not convenient — or safe — to disregard it. They ought, instead, to think of law as an attempt to describe the way to public safety and also the way to a private sense of self-fulfillment.

The idea of keeping the civil law because it is the policeman's law is similar to the idea of performing religious duty in the hope of escaping divine punishment. In both cases the individual forgets that the so-called duties of the law are but an outsider's way of looking at activities that the citizen and religious person consider privileges. To the conscientious citizen and to the devoutly religious, laws (whether civil or religious) are but expressions of freedom and liberty. It is a curious fact that men will so readily fight — and die if necessary — for liberty and yet still fail to exercise that liberty! But some explanation can be found in the mistaking of anarchy for freedom in the public order and license for liberty in the moral order.

If these mistakes are not made and if it is clear that laws are not imposed for restraining freedom, then more of the reason for our previously stated convictions can be seen. A moral obligation does exist toward the public order represented in the state.

And the democratic form of government, which allows people to govern themselves through their representatives as well as they can — or as poorly as they must — this form is a favorable one in society toward the development of personality.

The Objective of the Social Process

We return here to a familiar theme of these studies and state it as it relates to society. Persons as immortal souls are the ends, the real objectives, of the whole social process. As we have repeatedly said, every man is one for whom Christ died. Therefore every man is, or is supposed to be, not only a living being but also a growing, immortal soul — growing toward fulfillment as an individual living in society. The fact of growth is the essential characteristic to which we refer when we say that a thing lives; so also, the cessation of growth is the essential fact to which we refer when we say a thing is dead. Life, then, is never a finished product or an accomplished fact. Life is a process involving the achievement of ends or purposes — that is, growth. Likewise, death is not a finished state of affairs but is progressive decay. When death is finished, the object that is dead is nothing as an object.

These facts mean that all institutions of whatever kind among men must find their reason for existing in the contribution they are capable of making toward the growth of persons — toward the development of the conscious process of self-fulfillment of persons as immortal souls. The public order — government, civil society — is no exception to the truth of this principle!

By this time, having seen this principle restated several times in various ways, someone may wish to remind us what the Westminster Shorter Catechism declares concerning the purposes for man: "Man's chief end is to glorify God, and to enjoy him forever" (Question No. 1). With this statement we are in accord. For it seems to us that glorifying God does not mean genuflections, prostrations with face to the ground, or simply shouts or songs of adulation. Where such ideas of glorification exist, they seem to us to make God a despot or an Oriental potentate. Rather, to glorify God is to fulfill his purpose, and that purpose, as far as we can see, is the endless growth of persons as persons. Such growth is a process that involves one for all and all for each. It is a process in which, as Jesus said, losing life is a way to find it. (See Matt. 10:39.) This paradoxical statement is true because self-awareness is always awareness of oneself among other selves, including God as the ultimate person. Or the same truth can be expressed this way: self-fulfillment is always a by-product of activity which is admired by (or useful to) persons. So it is that the whole circle of relationships through which people grow as persons — through contact with one another and with the physical order (which physical contact is the means of personal intercommunication and relationship) — becomes the way to glorify God and the way to enjoy him.

THE PUBLIC ORDER AND PERSONAL MORAL OBLIGATION

Having stated something of the nature and importance of citizenship in the wider society beyond the family, we would conclude this chapter with some observations for practical problems confronting us in society.

No Public Order Could Be Perfect

No form of public order could achieve perfection — the democratic form or any other. Moreover, the democratic form, which we have said favors the development of persons, cannot be regarded as absolutely necessary to the development of persons. Political democracy and moral democracy are not the same thing, as we have already pointed out; moral democracy would be a state of society wherein full justice was provided for all. That the ideal form of government to achieve a moral democracy has yet been discovered is impossible to say. However, if there can be such a thing as an inalienable right that the ideal form of government is obligated to recognize, it may be argued that the right to freedom for the individual is such a right. But even here certain questions would have to be asked: " The freedom of what kind of persons? Within what sort of limits is this freedom to be exercised? "

Although we do not attempt here to discuss these questions, considerations such as these are of practical importance to the individual citizen in this way: they warn that one should not pass moral judgments on the basis of political and civic ideals. There is a constant temptation to do this. If we find ourselves in radical disagreement with a person regarding matters of social policy, we are likely to feel there is something wrong with his morals. Such charges are frequently leveled at social liberals by social and religious conservatives. The fact is that no form of public order is — or could be — perfect in the sense of being a final ideal. In a world where change and growth constitute the very meaning the word " person " is intended to convey, achieving such an ideal is impossible. Social and religious conservatives especially need to remember this lest they criticize on an improper basis the morals of those who seek changes in the social order.

The Moral Obligation to Support the Public Order

A moral obligation to support the public order exists. This fact stands in spite of the necessary imperfection of any public order. The state is not something apart from the people; it is the people organized for the accomplishment of certain objectives. The state is good in the sense that good objectives, not otherwise attainable, are thus possible of attainment. One can recognize this principle and yet say " the least government is the best government." Asserting that the least government is best cannot mean, of course, that the functions and services of government should never increase. This would limit the attainment of good objectives. It does mean that government should not be more complex and expensive than is necessary to achieve the good objectives.

The matter of the changing functions of government is one of several that the thoughtful citizen must consider as he recognizes a moral obligation to support the public order. Is the function of government simply to protect citizens from the invasion of rights recognized by the founding fathers? Or does the responsibility of government include more also?

Thomas Jefferson (1743–1826) is frequently quoted on this matter. He believed the rights of individuals could be divided into two groups. One group of rights coud be adequately supported by the individual himself. Thought, speech, religion, and the like were such rights. These the individual should be left free to maintain himself. Thus we have the constitutional provisions in our country for individual freedom in these regards. But Jefferson also believed the individual had a second group of rights that society must help the individual to maintain because he was not adequate for their defense himself. This group of rights included the right to property, freedom from personal attack, invasion, etc. A man through intelligence and industry could protect himself from want, for example, but he needed social protection against theft and murder.

This distinction of rights seemed valid in the days of the founding of our nation. But times have changed. Should governmental functions remain the same? Should the thoughtful citizen feel obligated to support changes or resist them? While we cannot answer the question, we must recognize as fact that it is increasingly difficult (if not impossible) to maintain Jefferson's distinction unchanged. Such freedoms as those of thought, speech, assembly, religion — or even of equality before the law — are scarcely freedoms at all if they must be exercised at the cost of a man's means of support for himself and his family. Increasingly, protection of the "freedom from want" has become a social demand upon the government. Any government officials, responsible to the wishes of the people, cannot long disregard public protection of this right and stay in office. Recognition of this particular problem has been in the "New Deal" and the "Forgotten Man" philosophy. Similarly, Dwight D. Eisenhower's philosophy asserted continuing liberalism where people are concerned, although conservatism where business is concerned.

Support of Public Order Must Not Surrender Individual Freedom

While we may acknowledge a moral obligation to support the public order, such support must not lead to the surrender of individual freedom. This is a danger. If one supports an acknowledged imperfect civic order, it may lead to surrender of his freedom to protest and his freedom to oppose the imperfect order. As an illustration of what we mean, we can take the changing attitude just mentioned toward governmental responsibility in the matter of freedom from want.

In today's society, some public help seems needed to assist the individual to protect this freedom. But — where "freedom from want" is substituted for "freedom of enterprise," and where this substitution becomes a major objective of public policy, there is a danger that the enterprise which has to supply freedom from want will be progressively unable to do so. The question is, "How far can a public policy of supplying wants go without destroying the only means of supplying them?" Here is one of the major battlegrounds of domestic politics. Here, also, is a major reason why absolutist theories of government dismiss democratic forms as impossible for survival.

Citizens cannot avoid involvement in this issue. The most they can hope for is to adopt a general principle on which to take a stand, and in the light of that principle be content with such changes as the public order decrees — so long as the principle itself is kept clear. But being content does not mean giving up the right to protest and to oppose encroachments on that freedom necessary to self-fulfillment. All legal and proper means must be used to keep the public consciousness alive to this basic need and right of the individual.

We suggest this general principle on which one can stand in spite of changes: freedom of activity is good; security in some measure is necessary to freedom — but security is a means, never an end in itself. Some measure of freedom must be sacrificed —

always and everywhere — in order to have security. But to obtain security at the cost of complete freedom would be total disaster. Freedom of activity is essential. Consciously worthwhile activity is the sole source from which meaning in life arises. Life is not a "something" or an "it." Surrender of all freedom would lead to surrender of life itself as a meaningful activity.

If this general principle is followed, then obviously the limits to freedom can never be fixed once for all. The limitations on freedom and the gaining of security will have to change with the changing circumstances, as those circumstances change out of which a sense of self-fulfillment can arise. Opinions will always vary as to which changes are wise in a social order if everybody is to have a just measure of opportunity for self-fulfillment. Opinions will vary as to how much freedom and how much security is necessary. Such differences of opinion provide the safeguard against too little or too great a change in the public order.

Change in the public order is inevitable. Life and growth are synonymous; and the public order is an order of living, growing — and thus changing — beings. The unchanging principle behind the changing public order is this: security is only a means; freedom of activity is the end good. Activity is necessary to meaningful self-fulfillment. On this basis one can support the public order while not surrendering his ultimate individual freedom.

Patriotism as a Moral Duty

Our conclusion is that patriotism is a moral duty. A citizen should support the public order as a moral obligation. By this we do not mean that the public order should be maintained in a static form. Neither the Constitution nor the present interpretation of it is completely sacrosanct. Changes have been made and will be made. The patriotic citizen cannot prevent change and should not wish to do so, since change is the way of life and of living things. But — he *should* seek to exert his influence so that the changes will be in a direction that will maintain and further the freedom which is necessary to his sense of self-fulfillment. In our day of unlimited power and of world-embracing mass movements, the danger is that the patriot will surrender freedom voluntarily to a government in the hope of receiving security in return. In such surrender he is encouraged by the sense of individual helplessness in the face of material and social forces that envelop us all. So the patriotic citizen must be on guard concerning those changes to which he gives his consent and influence.

If a citizen wishes to be moral, he cannot withhold his efforts on behalf of the public order. Some citizens attempt to do so on the grounds that they disagree with what is going on or on the grounds that they dislike politics and politicians. Three things need to be remembered in this connection.

In the first place, there are reasons why the public order is as it is and became the way it is. If one is dissatisfied, one cannot begin to make things better except by beginning with the public order as it is at present. Certainly social chaos would not be a better place to start; and chaos would result if all who disagreed refused to support the present public order. This is where those are wrong who refuse to support public officials whose election they opposed or refuse to obey laws that they did not approve. The real need is to see that *any* organized order is better than chaos. In every case, what exists at present becomes, in an important sense, the basis for improvement. What is cannot be cast aside in the hope of a completely new start.

We have already said that there can be no perfect human order. So the second thing to remember is akin to the first. Waiting for a *wholly* approved order before participating actively as citizens becomes silent participation in what is disapproved. This is where such groups as those who call themselves "pacifists" are wrong. I do not mean to say that such persons are guilty of sin before God. Their sincerity is very often both genuine and admirable, and nobody is liable to God's judgment so long as he does what he sincerely thinks he ought. But such persons are nevertheless wrong — wrong in the same sense that a person is wrong who follows an unenlightened conscience in any action.

A perfect human order is a "flying goal"—an ideal that reshapes itself. Every intellectual and social achievement is attained by such reshaping in the light of progress made in the past. There can be no such thing as a perfect order of human beings that is achieved and finished. The situation is like that of a mountain climber whose horizon expands with every step of upward progress. Even heaven itself, if it is a living state, must be a place to grow and achieve; it is not merely a finished state wherein nothing further is possible. So there is no point in simply waiting inactively for the establishment of a perfect human order. Approach to such an order requires active effort toward it.

This suggests the third thing that ought to be remembered. One's functioning in a social order is what brings about the sense of self-fulfillment in the individual. The *in*ability to function meaningfully causes frustration. The sense of self-fulfillment arises as one is aware of activity that is worth-while when he judges it in the light of the ideals he cherishes or the goals he seeks to reach. This is true in regard to participation in the public order as elsewhere. So inactivity in the public order because of disagreements or dislikes is not the solution to one's problem, even though the activity may seem to offer but small chance of bringing about a change toward one's ideal. In the field of personal, moral, and social attainment, one does not have to change things so much as he has to learn the secrets discovered by the apostle Paul. For one thing, Paul discovered that God works for good in all things with those who love him; and for another thing, that for himself he had become able to be content—not with—but *in* whatever state he found himself. (See Rom. 8:28 and Phil. 4:11.) The public order provides the field for such discovery, and nowhere is the situation so dismal as to make this discovery impossible.

CHAPTER

VIII

Looking Ahead

Moral problems are real and they are permanent. I cannot imagine a time to come when people will feel that such problems have been largely solved. Of course this does not mean that progress is impossible. It means only that as advances are made, discernment also increases; the need for further achievement continues to be apparent. The situation in which we must live will always be a problem situation as long as natural human dispositions remain as they are. Desire, passion, and selfishness will continue to involve people in troublesome moral decisions.

Likewise, moral codes with specific requirements will continue to become inadequate. This will be true not because what present codes require no longer matters but because what they require is not inclusive enough to meet the new and changing situations of the future. An example of this can be seen by comparing *past* moral codes with *present* situations. How does one apply the old moral injunction " Thou shalt not kill " to a social order in which it has become a national necessity to prepare for total destruction by hydrogen bomb warfare? This is a question that citizens must face when they vote. No longer do people harm one another chiefly in face-to-face relationships. The old moral code seems inadequate, and who can predict the moral demands on future generations?

While we must recognize the reality and permanency of moral problems such as those above, we must not overlook, on the other hand, that the character of a person is still formed chiefly in face-to-face relationships as it always has been. A man's character becomes known in face-to-face expressions of kindness, integrity, sincerity, industry, etc. We judge ourselves, and we are judged by others, in such face-to-face relationships. As we have previously suggested, to immerse oneself completely in mass movements and to reflect only the mass mind is to cease being an individual person. When we wish to judge a man's attitude in other than face-to-face relationships, we must resort to the character traits that have been established in his personal relationships.

WHAT WE CAN DO

As we consider these facts and look ahead — for the future begins *now* — what shall we do? Some practical suggestions in answer to that question can be allowed to bring this series of brief studies in morals to a close.

Judge Morals by Progress in a Direction

One thing we can do is this: we can begin to judge our moral actions in terms of progress in a direction. In spite of the difficulty of the moral problems facing us, the times do not call for pessimism. On the contrary, no generation has ever lived that had a conception of what is worth-while equal to the conception we have. Think of the vast knowledge we have of man's capacities! Think of the resources available in the world as we know it for the achievement of those capacities! No generation has ever known better what ought to be and could be. We know what is worth living for and what is worth dying for. So, knowing the direction in which men ought to move, we know the direction in which to spend our efforts. So also, we can judge our actions morally according to our progress in that direction.

But let us be clear about living and dying. Nobody ought to jump at the opportunity to die for a great cause, only at the chance to live for a worthy cause. Sacrifice for its own sake is never justifiable. This is a principle that everybody, especially young people, ought always to keep in mind. Life is good; happiness is good. Only a great cause could warrant a great sacrifice such as that. And even a great cause cannot warrant a heedless or wasteful expenditure of life — life that is the highest good. Since we know better than any previous generation could know what is good and what is possible, then as long as action in this direction is possible for us, the good life can never be denied to us.

Our moral duty in any situation is simply the best we can do in that situation. Our duty is always that which is immediately at hand; never a distant, impossible goal. Each of us can be sure that progress will be made as he does his own job well. Of course, each needs to be as intelligent as he can be about the problems facing the world, but this need is only because he requires the knowledge in order to do his job well. Knowledge, after all, is not a warehouse full of books. Knowledge as books is only ink and paper. Knowledge is knowing; and knowing is awareness of what has been, is, and may be. Therefore, the knowledge that we need is to the end and purpose of work well done.

Work well done is done where we live. A "citizen of the world" must exercise his citizenship in specific relationships. And in such specific relationships, what to do next is usually clear enough. If I am to cast my vote for justice and tolerance in the world, I must cast it in my own voting precinct. The duty of a good citizen has never been expressed better than by the prophet Jeremiah when he addressed a message to captives swept away before a deeply entrenched and evil power. He said, "Seek the welfare of the city where I have sent you into exile, and pray to the Lord on its behalf, for in its welfare you will find your welfare." (Jer. 29:7. But see vs. 4 ff.) The magnitude of world problems today must not be allowed to obscure the fact that our duty is in the place where we live. Here, progress is possible and immediate duty — duty during the next moment, which is all we really have — is clearly discernible. Here, moral actions can be judged in terms of immediate duty toward the direction of the known good.

Persons Are the Purpose

Another thing we can do is this: We can open our eyes to the fact that the purpose of the scheme of things is persons. This realization will greatly affect what we do and how we act in life. When we see this fact we shall see that the purpose of our being is to help others become worthy persons. But also with that, the purpose is to become the best possible persons ourselves. God's purpose in history is not history but persons. He is concerned with personal character, not with events as events. So long as the conditions in which we live make character development possible, it is correct to say that God's purpose in us can be fulfilled regardless of what events may come to pass. The writer of Ecclesiastes said it this way: "So I saw that there is nothing better than that a man should enjoy his work, for that is his lot; who can bring him to see what will be after him?" (Eccl. 3:22.)

People often become immensely excited about events in history. They are deeply concerned that God shall bring certain events to pass in history. Now of course, what comes to pass in history is vastly important. One cannot deny that truth. But, we must keep in mind that events which come to pass in history simply record what men and women do. The *doing* is the important thing. Events in history are not events apart from the deeds of those who achieve them and are affected by them. This means then, if our particular doing does not greatly change the onflowing stream of events — which may very well be true because we are too few or too small — we shall still live well so long as what we do is worth doing.

Take, for example, the matter of sacrifices. I have sometimes heard people say that the sacrifices our young men have made in recent wars — hot and cold — appear to have been useless in view of the continuing state of the world. Such people are judging the sacrifices in the light of whether or not those for whom they were made have had the intelligence to profit by those sacrifices. But this is not the proper way to judge a sacrifice. A sacrifice must be judged by the fact that it was made. Even the world's perfect sacrifice, that of Christ, cannot be judged perfect in the sense that all for whom it was made have availed themselves of the freedom it provides. Christ's sacrifice was perfect in the sense that he made it and in the sense that all might benefit from it. The benefits — real benefits — we derive from a sacrifice are a matter of our own choosing. But, our choosing is no measure of the perfection, or worth, of another's sacrifice. Not one's ability to become recorded in history but one's ability to do that which he believes is worth-while — that determines whether one is living well and fulfilling real purpose.

When we consider giving ourselves to support some cause, we need not condition our willingness to do our part by the degree of assurance we feel that our abilities will be enough to guarantee success for the cause. If the cause is considered better than the other causes that provide us with live options for our activity, and if the program of activity we choose to follow is the best we can do, then we shall not miss the good life no matter how events may turn out. God's concern with history is not history, but personality — character. Life is not made by events; it is made by persons. What persons do may become events in history. Personal activity becomes history when — and if — a sufficient number of people do that which causes changes sweeping enough to be worthy of record as possibly useful information for later generations. Still, nobody should judge the righteousness of the direction of his activity merely by the numbers of people headed that way.

Moral Hope

A third thing we can do is this: believe in certain things that in sum add up to moral hope for the future instead of moral pessimism. We are clearly entitled to such belief.

We are entitled to believe in the ability of life in general to find conscious fulfillment in almost any conceivable course of events which may be ahead of us. These are tremendously stimulating times in which to be alive. I have sometimes said that even if it were our lot to see our world blown up and disintegrated in a mighty *wh-h-h-o-o-sh,* it would still be a thrilling experience to carry with us into immortality. What a conversation piece that would be in heaven!

Joking aside, we must not allow ourselves to forget that it is the nature of life to adapt itself and to fulfill its essential functions in widely varying circumstances. I have seen barrel cactus in full bloom in the hot, dry soil of the Mesa Verde in southwestern Colorado. I have watched a healthy young paulownia (princess tree) on our campus. It is growing from a hole in a gnarled old cedar tree. At a spot in the cedar higher than my head, it has split the cedar's trunk wide asunder as its roots and stem have searched for moisture and room to grow. We accept as a normal characteristic in living things such growth as this; we call it adaptation.

Human life too — our lives — has resources for adaptation and fulfillment not easily defeated. We do well to remember that the record of good men's lives is more than an account of favorable fortune. The secret of worthy living is not favorable fortune and length of days but a present right direction and a stout heart. So we have reason to hope for the future.

We are entitled also to believe in people. The person who has " lost faith in mankind " does not really know whereof he speaks. Of course some men are vicious. Many are weak. Many are ignorant. But a great many are good and strong also. To be unaware of that, one must be blind indeed. One meets such people everywhere.

During many summer vacations I have driven, with such members of my family as were available, across many sections of this country. These experiences have provided a never-failing lift and renewal of faith in people. From an automobile window as homes, fields, churches, schools, and towns glide past, the view reminds one of the hopes, the courage and faith, the toil and sacrifice, that such things represent. A small, rather pathetic, country church, with its brave little spire and its poor dead bell, reminds one of the aspirations of those whose willing hands have tried to fashion small gifts into a temple fit for the presence of God.

I have found too that people are friendly. To be sure, they often swear. In some respects they appear rough, sometimes uncouth. But almost always they have provided help if I required it. They have given directions. They have engaged in friendly talk if I have wished to talk. They have laughed at a joke and frequently responded with a merry word of their own. Surely all this is title enough to justify faith in people. Not title enough to justify expectation of great wisdom or heroic stature but enough to justify faith in fundamental soundness.

Yes, we are entitled to believe in those things which add up to moral hope for the future.

Defend and Build on Present Values

Another thing we can do is this: we can accept the fact that the values which have been incorporated into our way of life must be defended. This is not because such ways are perfect, but because (as already stated) they provide the starting place for progress; there is no other choice. The future starts now; the place it starts from is here. Need for great improvement no doubt exists; radical changes in certain areas are doubtless required. But just the same, no other public order we can presently envision provides so good a foundation as our own provides for men, standing in their turn, to build a worthy future for themselves and their children, just as our fathers built for themselves and for us in bringing us to the place where we now stand.

Who knows whether the way of living we call "the good life" can be made a prevailing order? Could it be proved that love is the supreme fact of the universe? Could it be proved that a social order based on brotherhood would provide shelter and the other necessities for all people? The answers will have to be "No." But—the good life as we see it ought to be lived for its own sake and for our sake. The actual process of living well (according to our growing understanding of what living well means) gives the good order of things the only conscious reality it can ever have.

Moral Conclusions Are Principles and Guides to Conduct

Finally, we can do this: we can take our moral conclusions—honestly arrived at through earnest and reverent study—as principles to live by. We can use them as guides to conduct. Doing this, we shall find ourselves approving truth and condemning falsehood. We shall approve honor and condemn dishonor; we shall approve devotion to the good in personal and civic relations and shall hate crime and treason. All such conclusions are easy to reach; they are deeply embedded in the culture that has shaped us, the common mores or morals. We need no elaborate intellectual defense of them. And regardless of happenings in our world that might suggest questions about the expediency of our conclusions, nothing has happened to suggest more valid principles.

We can be guided by principles such as these. By following them, the resulting good qualities will be embodied in our living. And these qualities constitute what we are accustomed to think of as integrity of character. These good qualities *are* possible in us; men and women no wiser or stronger, no more fortunately situated than we are, have been guided by such principles in the past. Such principles have been the cement that made the social structure possible; they have made life endurable. Take, for example, the principle of truth; society could not exist without it. If nobody could be depended upon to tell the truth, all reason for social intercommunication would be gone. Society would collapse. Or the principle of loyalty. If nobody could be depended upon for loyalty to the church or the state, social anarchy and chaos would result.

In other words, we are speaking of qualities—behavior characteristics—that motivate integrating, instead of disintegrating, social relationships. Such characteristics in an individual constitute him a person, since a person cannot exist in the complete absence of all social relationships. Social relationships are the very fabric of life, whether on earth or in heaven. Integrating relationships cause persons to be persons according to the same principle in material nature that causes objects to become objects. Integration is the one most important fact in the universe. Material objects or living things as we know them would not exist without integration. The maple tree outside my window is such a marvel of co-operative functioning or integration. I know that it would be scientifically possible to reduce its various parts to a vast network of small units of material. Each unit functions in accordance with laws that a scientist could state with mathematical exactitude. But such reduction to parts would not leave me with a tree. The functioning together of the parts makes the tree whose beauty I enjoy as I look out my window.

So it is with everything.

CONCLUSION

This fact of integration — co-operative functioning, mutuality — is the most important characteristic of things in nature. To the extent that integration is characteristic of people, they become persons; they create societies. All this provides reason enough to justify the conviction that persons are the real purpose of the whole scheme of things. One cannot possibly imagine a wholly purposeless process or scheme of things. The fact that a process brings about an end or fulfills a purpose enables us to regard it as a process, i.e., a proceeding in an orderly manner. It is equally impossible for us to imagine the scheme of things as having no other purpose than the scheme of things itself. That amounts to denial of the very intelligence that enables us to see that there is a discernible scheme of things.

Thus we have said that we cannot imagine a higher purpose in the universe than the purpose to create persons. Thus we have said that God's interest in history is not history but persons. And moreover, since this is so, God can have no plans or purposes for any future generation that he does not wish to see fulfilled in this. We become the means to the fulfillment of God's purpose in creation only as we realize in ourselves the end of his purpose also. No man is more truly "the man for whom Christ died" than I am, or than you are. As far as we can see, the cause and purpose of the universe is that we, and others like us, should become living, growing, immortal persons. And we believe that those characteristics to which we refer when we use such words as goodness, truth, justice, and their like are the means to the end of our becoming persons in this true sense.

It seems strange, when one stops to think about it, that it is so difficult for us to be contented with the simple qualities that constitute personality as an eternal, spiritual real. I sometimes sit in the church where I go to worship, gaze at the beautiful window behind the chancel, and ask myself why this difficulty troubles us. The central panel of the window contains, as its chief figure, the artist's conception of the face and form of Jesus. On either side stand the writers of the Gospels: Matthew, Mark, Luke, and John. In the panels below and above are pictured scenes taken from the life of Jesus as recorded in the Gospels. They are scenes of simple, uncomplicated human helpfulness. They represent what Jesus did *after* he had grown to full stature — *after* he had "increased in wisdom and in stature, and in favor with God and man" (Luke 2:52). If such actions were enough in his case, why would they not be enough in mine? In those surroundings I have said that it is enough. And when the organ plays, I bow my head and say: "It is enough. I'll try to follow this simple way."

Some years ago, just before the beginning of a Christmas holiday vacation at college, a final Christmas vesper service was held on a Sunday evening under the direction of the combined musical organizations of the college. It was an inspiring and moving experience. But as I walked away from the building afterward, my wife and I overheard a student talking with a companion as they also walked away. He said: "I'm getting tired of this Christmas stuff. This d— religion gets you after a while. You can take only just so much; then it sort of gets you. You know, sort of gets you."

I think I understand something of why this lad felt as he did. He was a man grown up — in height and weight, at least — with a man's emotions and desires. This Christmas stuff "got him" because it seemed so irrelevant to his life. The music seemed to be concerned with lambs and babies and angels with wings and stars and incense and halos and kneeling down and saying prayers and singing praise. But how does all that fit into this kind of world? How does it help resolve the world's confusion? He was a young man. He had a young man's strength and a young man's clamoring desires so impatient with delay. He wanted to get on with the real business of living. So he had become fed up with the sentimental — the figurative. I can very well understand him.

But this lad was wrong nevertheless! He was missing, at least momentarily, what the "Christmas stuff" was all about. He was bogged down in the figurative. He had not translated the figurative into its appropriate meanings. So he had failed where many another fails: the *meaning* of the symbolism explains everything. The meaning is a very simple truth.

The truth that all the symbolism of Christmas intends to convey is simply this: the universe is friendly and good! — friendly as the marvelous gift of a new baby is a sign of friendliness; good as the care of a mother is good. No one can really tire of assurance of friendliness and goodness in the universe. Such assurance is our real basis for confidence and for the feeling of security we have as we try to help in the erection of places of security where persons — immortal souls — can live and grow. Only with such assurance do we confidently form homes, churches, communities, and nations wherein persons can become more and more the children of God in fact, as they are even now in promise.

The greatest single fact we know in the universe is that ultimate substances work together to produce the material universe and people work together to produce persons. In this sense the universe is friendly toward good; it is friendly toward the development of persons. This is good in the sense intended in Gen. 1:31, where it is said, "God saw everything that he had made, and behold, it was very good." So the ethical and religious expression of the friendly spirit serves to put us in touch with the very nature of the Real. This truth we must not forget.